James West Stack

South Island Maoris

A Sketch of Their History and Legendary Lore

James West Stack

South Island Maoris
A Sketch of Their History and Legendary Lore

ISBN/EAN: 9783744733458

Printed in Europe, USA, Canada, Australia, Japan

Cover: Foto ©ninafisch / pixelio.de

More available books at **www.hansebooks.com**

South Island Maoris

*A SKETCH OF THEIR HISTORY
AND
LEGENDARY LORE.*

BY

CANON STACK.

Christchurch, Wellington, Dunedin and Auckland:
WHITCOMBE & TOMBS LIMITED

Dedication.

I DEDICATE THIS SKETCH OF MAORI TRADITIONS

TO THE

PRESIDENT AND MEMBERS

OF THE

Christchurch Savage Club,

IN ACKNOWLEDGMENT OF THE INTEREST SHEWN

BY THEM IN ALL MATTERS RELATING

TO THE HISTORY AND CUSTOMS OF THE

MAORI PEOPLE.

CHRISTCHURCH,
    October, 1898.

PREFACE.

The Maoris of New Zealand are a portion of a race which shares with two other races—the Papuan and Malay—the countless islands of the Pacific. The chief centres of Maori population are found in the Hawaiian, Samoan, Rarotongan and New Zealand Islands.

The language spoken by the New Zealanders is a dialect of the language common to all branches of the Maori race. The extreme simplicity of its structure is a proof of its great antiquity. The grammar is peculiar as compared with the ancient and modern languages of Europe. Nouns are not inflected nor the verbs conjugated in the same way. To form the cases or the plurals of nouns, or the mood, tense, or person, of a verb, all that is required is to put a participle before or after the word. There is no auxiliary verb "to be," but its place is supplied by a participle. The pronouns are very complete and possess double duals and double plurals.

The vocabulary is wanting in words to express abstract ideas, but full of terms to describe outward objects. But there are here and there words which seem to indicate that abstract ideas were once more familiar to the minds of the race than they are now. But while the language is defective for the purpose of argumentative discourse, it is peculiarly well adapted for the purpose of narration and the peculiar style of oratory cultivated by the people.

The art of writing was unknown till it was introduced by the English missionaries about the year 1820. It was by the advice of Professor Lee, of Cambridge, that Roman letters were employed to represent the sounds of the language, and a phonetic system of spelling adopted in forming the words. Only fourteen letters are used to express the sounds of the dialect spoken by the New Zealanders—five vowels and nine consonants, none of which are sibilants. This is a noticeable peculiarity as sibilants do exist in the Samoan, Rarotongan and Hawaiian dialects. Except in forming the sound *Nga* no two consonants ever come together, and every syllable and every word ends in a vowel, which renders the language when spoken soft and euphonious.

The local differences of dialect in New Zealand though important in the estimation of the natives appear trivial to us, being nothing like as great as the differences which exist between the dialects of the northern and western counties of England.

The South Islanders substituted *K* for *Nga*, in the same way that the Hawaiians and most other Polynesians do. Instead of pronouncing the word for village as if spelt Kainga, it was pronounced as if spelt *Kaika*; but I have not thought it advisable to adopt this local peculiarity when spelling the Maori words which occur in the following pages. I have preferred to spell them as they will be found spelt in all standard books printed in the Maori tongue.

The letters of the Maori alphabet are :—

A	pronounced as *a* in father		O	pronounced	O
E	,,	as *a* in acorn	P	,,	pa
H	,,	ha	R	,,	ra
I	,,	as *ee* in sleep	T	,,	ta
K	,,	ka	U	,,	as *oo* in too
M	,,	ma	W	,,	wa
N	,,	na	Nga	,,	as ngah

When pronouncing a Maori word, the reader must be careful to sound every vowel distinctly.

I regret that I have been unable to obtain photographs of the sites of the ancient pas which can still be recognised by the earth works which protected them, such as O te Kaue, at the mouth of the Wairau River, Waipapa, Kahutara, Waikouaiti, etc. I have been unable, too, to procure a correct picture of a Maori fortress as it existed before the period of colonization. It was a structure as unlike anything to be seen in this country now as a Norman castle was unlike a modern English villa.

The war canoe shewn on page 47 does not represent the largest of the sea-going canoes, which were longer, wider and deeper than this modern specimen.

The portrait of Pita Te Hori found on page 36 is worthy of special notice, as it is the likeness of the last Tohunga, or learned chief, of Ngaitahu. It was from him that I obtained most of my knowledge of South Island tribal lore.

I would recommend those of my readers who wish to obtain more information about the subjects referred to in the following pages, to read Sir George Grey's book on "Polynesian Mythology;" "Old Pakeha Maori," by Judge Manning; Yates' "New Zealand;" Dr. Shortland's Works; "Ika-a-maui," by Rev. R. Taylor; and the admirable series of papers on Maori habits and customs contributed by the Rev. W. Colenso to the "Transactions of New Zealand Institute."

I am largely indebted to the writings of the late Sir George Grey for the contents of the last chapter of this publication; and while acknowledging how much I owe to him, I wish to point out to my readers how greatly all New Zealanders are indebted to our late Governor for rescuing from oblivion the most interesting and most valuable portion of the Maori traditions which we possess. In a letter which I received from him in February, 1892, he told me how he first became acquainted with the story of Hinemoa; and the account given by him is so interesting that I feel that it would be an act of injustice to him not to publish it. "I think," he wrote, "you may be interested to know that the story was not as you seem to suppose, committed to writing by a Maori chief, but was written down by myself under the following circumstances:—

"On Wednesday, December 26th, 1849, I was on a pedestrian tour from Auckland to Wellington (we were then compelled to make all land journeys on foot; there were no roads, and, I may say, no horses in the interior; we often suffered from fatigue and hunger).

"With some of my party I was on the island of Mokoia, but I wandered away alone, accompanied by three or four old chiefs. We sat down to rest on the rocky edge of a hot spring shaded by Pohutukawa trees--the bath that Hinemoa had swum to. My constant work was collecting old poems and legends. The chiefs knew this, and began to tell me the story of Hinemoa. I saw that it was a thing of beauty and got them to repeat the tale; and then by questioning them, obtained it fully with all its details as it stands now. When I got back with my party to the mainland to dine with the good and hospitable missionary Mr. Chapman, I related briefly to him the tale at dinner. He said I had been deceived; if there was such a tale he must have heard it, as he had lived there for several years. He was so excited that he got up from his dinner and went out to speak to some of the natives; returned and said he found I was right. I then took considerable pains with the translation, choosing the most fitting words to convey the meaning of the Maori original, and to convey the spirit and sense of the original; and the tale was published early in 1851 with my translation in a Maori newspaper, and taken from that and published in a little journal of my journey overland, published in Auckland in 1851. My translation of the tale was published in 1855, by Murray, in my "Polynesian Mythology."

"From that time many persons writing of New Zealand, have introduced the tale without any acknowledgement, and it became a favourite exercise to produce a translation of it which should excel mine—which I have never touched since I first wrote it. Amongst others, Manning, who was a great Maori scholar, in 1870 or 1871 published an English version of the tale ; and Lord Pembroke, in his writings, attributes the discovery of it to Manning. In this manner the discovery of the tale has been attributed to several people, many of whose translations were perhaps better than mine. The only credit I claim is having probably rescued it from loss or corruption ; and for having by questions and interest shewn, elicited niceties of thought and expression which could not perhaps have been drawn out by others. These remarks apply equally to the tale of Ponga to which you also allude."

I am painfully aware that this publication has suffered from the haste with which its materials have been put together ; a haste necessitated by my approaching departure from the colony ; but the readiness with which Messrs. Whitcombe & Tombs have kindly undertaken to publish it for me at short notice, and the remembrance of the favourable reception given a few years back to my story of "Kaiapohia," has emboldened me to ask the public to accept, in spite of its defects, this small contribution to Maori history, and the attempt I have made in it to correct some of the erroneous opinions which are current regarding the character and attainments of the Maori people.

JAMES W. STACK.

The Vicarage, Fendalton,
    Canterbury, New Zealand.

CONTENTS.

PREFACE—   PAGE
  Maori Language.
  Rules regarding pronunciation.
  Sir George Grey's letter *re* Hinemoa.

CHAPTER I.—
  Sources of information 9
  Difficulty of unravelling thread of the history 13
  Chronology 14

CHAPTER II.—FABULOUS TRADITIONS—
  Rongo, The Strider 15
  Tama, circumnavigator 19
  Ogre of Molyneux 20

CHAPTER III.—UNCERTAIN TRADITIONS
  Waitaha 22
  Tutewaimate and Moko .. 25
  Destruction of large bird of prey 26
  Ngatimamoe till 1677 28
  Connection with Chathams .. 29

CHAPTER IV.—RELIABLE TRADITIONS—
  Ngaitahu 30
  Causes which led to their migration from the North Island 31
  Maoris from west coast, North Island 32
  Tutekawa 38
  Last migration 41
  Commencement of war with Ngatimamoe 43
  Marus leniency 44
  Waitai's defection .. 44
  Naval engagement .. 45
  Battle of Ika a Whaturoa 49
  Capture of Waipapa 55
  Battle of Opokihi 56
  Battle of Kahutara 56
  Raid on Omihi .. 57
  Rangitauneke's duel 60
  Death of Manawa 64
  Siege of Pakihi .. 68
  Occupation of Caves 68
  The Maiden of Taiari 69
  Te Wera 71

CHAPTER V.—   PAGE
  Turakautahi's sons arrive .. 72
  Taking possession of the land .. 73
  Tutekawa's death 74
  West coast natives' discovery of greenstone 76
  Ngaitahu Expedition against West Coast 78
  Raid on the South .. 80
  Great Battle of Teihoka .. 82
  Tarewai 84
  Final destruction of Ngatimamoe .. 86
  Internal dissensions 89

CHAPTER VI.—MYTHOLOGY, ANCIENT HISTORY, LEGENDS AND POETRY, ETC., ETC.—
  Rangi and Papa 91
  Maui 93
  Tawhake 97
  Ancient home in Hawaiki .. 101
  Origin of the name Hawaiki .. 103
  How Maoris got to New Zealand .. 104
  Pleasing traits in Maori character .. 109
  Hinemoa 111
  Te Ponga and Puhihuia .. 114
  Fairies 117
  Magical wooden head 118
  Taniwhas 120
  Poetry 122
  Proverbs 129
  Proofs of refinement of feeling and intelligence 133

ILLUSTRATIONS.

Maori chief .. .. frontispiece
Figure-head of Maori canoe .. 16
Pita Te Hori 36
War canoes 47
Maori ladies 63
Greenstone ornament .. 79
Specimens of carved boxes, etc. 95
Whatas or storehouses .. 105
Specimens of carved sternposts 119

SOUTH ISLAND MAORIS.

Chapter I.

THIS sketch of the History of the South Island Maoris from the commencement of their occupation of the country until Ngai Tahu became established as the rulers of it, is intended to complete the accounts of the Ngai Tahu tribe which have already appeared in the author's Stories of Kaiapohia and Banks Peninsula.

The materials for this sketch were collected between 1859 and 1863, from native chiefs residing in different parts of the island, who were recognized by their fellow countrymen as authorities upon all questions relating to the history of the Maori race. The knowledge which they possessed had been handed down to them by tradition. But as the reliability of any oral tradition may fairly be questioned, I will endeavour to show why these may be considered worthy of credit, and also how in the absence of a written language, the Maoris were enabled accurately to preserve their history. Classes for instruction in the various subjects of knowledge cultivated by the people existed in every tribe. These classes, which were held in a building specially set apart for the purpose, called the Whare-pu-rakau, or Armoury, were opened annually with great ceremony at the beginning of winter, the date being fixed by the rising of Puaka (Rigel), a star in the constellation of Orion, which took place between May and June.

The classes were kept open for about three months. Instruction was imparted by a band of "tohungas," or skilled persons. The subjects taught comprised the myths relating to the origin of all things, and to the gods and demigods, the religious beliefs of the race, charms and incantations, the rules of "tapu," legends, fables, history (national and tribal), laws, genealogies, treatment of diseases, astronomy, agriculture, etc. The most proficient of the pupils trained in these schools formed the learned class, from which the "tohungas" were from time to time chosen.

To Europeans whose memories have not been exercised and trained to the same extent that the Maoris memories were, it seems almost incredible that so large an amount of knowledge on such a variety of subjects could have been preserved for any length of time by oral tradition ; but a comparison of the most ancient traditions of the Maoris of New Zealand with those of other branches of their race scattered over the Pacific, from all intercourse with whom they had been cut off for many centuries, proves that they have been correctly handed down, as they are identical in every particular point. "You white men," the Maoris say, "keep your knowledge on your bookshelves, we carry it about with us in our memories"

Every tribe was composed of hapus, and every hapu of families. Each family, hapu, and iwi carefully preserved the names of their ancestors, and their ancestors' wives and offspring. In transmitting this knowledge, the greatest care was taken to avoid errors, because, as the Maoris were very punctilious in the matter of precedence, a mistake made on the occasion of any public assembly of the tribes might be construed into an insult, and result in a blood feud. Such mistakes were all the more likely to happen from the custom which prevailed, when speaking of a chief, of alluding to him as a relation— "Brother, uncle, son, grandson, nephew, brother-in-law," etc., etc. A very accurate knowledge of tribal genealogies was therefore required to enable a speaker to apply to any given person that term which exactly described the rank to which he was entitled in the tribe. This knowledge was not confined to a class of learned genealogists, but was possessed by every rangatira or native gentleman. To acquire it, each one from childhood up was obliged to make this subject a constant study; and the public recitals which were held at frequent intervals kept the names and the facts connected with them always fresh in their memories; for, besides the names of their ancestors it was held to be of equal importance to know the deeds for which they were distinguished. The value attached by the Maoris to land is too well known. From the time that the first arrivals from Hawaiki ascended the highest mountains to partition all the country they could see from thence amongst themselves, the title to land has been a fruitful source of strife. Every part of the country was owned and named. Not only were the large mountains, rivers, and plains named, but every hillock, streamlet, and valley. These names frequently contained allusions to persons or events, and thus served to perpetuate the memory of them and to preserve the history of the past. Every Maori was required to know by what title the land claimed by his tribe was held, whether by right of original occupation, conquest, purchase, or gift; and thus it happened that traditions relating to the same transactions were preserved by tribes whose interests were antagonistic; and several opportunities have been afforded in recent times of comparing these accounts, which have been transmitted for several generations through separate and independent channels, and they have invariably been found to agree. With this fact before us, it is hardly possible to deny the historical value of a large portion of these traditions which have been preserved by the same method but which cannot be vouched for in the same manner.

I experienced considerable difficulty at first in disentangling the complicated narratives, because my Maori informants being themselves so familiar with the history did not see the necessity of explaining as they went along why things happened as they did. They would repeatedly break off from the continuous history of the tribe to follow the fortunes of a favourite hero, and again as abruptly leave him to resume the thread of the original narrative. One prolific source of confusion arose from the intermarriages which took place between the members of hostile tribes. It was bewildering to find the same person fighting for one tribe but wishing success to the other, and guilty of treachery towards both. The man who married a Ngatimamoe woman would be found plotting the ruin of his wife's relations; and the Ngaitmamoe man who, by marriage with a Ngai Tahu woman, was admitted to that tribe, would still sympathize with his own people, and betray his connections whenever he could. Another element of confusion arose from the two tribes being spoken of as totally distinct from each other, whereas they had a common origin, and this fact afforded the only explanation of many strange things done on either side. The history throughout is one dark narrative of treachery and ferocity, brightened here and there by displays of great courage and occasional acts of generosity.

The method I have adopted for ascertaining the chronological order in which the various events occurred, has been first to form a genealogical table, and then allowing *twenty years for a generation, to count back the generations from the present time, and thus fix the date of any event by the position in the table which the persons connected with it occupy. Of course this plan only gives an approximate date, but it is sufficiently near to render the history intelligible, though further investigation may lead to some alteration being made here and there in the sequence of events.

The history may be divided into four periods:
- 1st. Prior to the arrival of Waitaha.
- 2nd. Waitaha occupation, 1477 to 1577.
- 3rd. Ngatimamoe occupation, 1577 to 1677.
- 4th. Ngai Tahu occupation, 1677 to 1827 (the date of Rauparaha's invasion).

---

*I have fixed on twenty years, as the Maoris married early.

Chapter II.

THE traditions may be divided into three classes:—The Fabulous, the Uncertain, and the Reliable. The Fabulous relate to prehistoric times, and to supernatural beings; the Uncertain relate to those tribes which have perished, and whose only memorial is contained in the fragmentary notices which occur in the history of those who superseded and survive them; the Reliable comprise the history of Ngai Tahu during the last two hundred years.

The Fabulous traditions relate to the KAHUI TIPUA or band of ogres, a mythical race who are said to have been the first occupants of this island. They are described as giants who could stride from mountain range to mountain range, swallow rivers, and transform themselves into anything animate or inanimate that they choose.

When RONGO-I-TUA (Fame-from-afar) arrived from Hawaiki, he found the country inhabited by these ogres, who on seeing the stranger, ordered food to be set before him; their servants brought specimens of all their choicest delicacies, but Rongo hardly tasted anything, and presently asked for a bowl of water to be brought. This

Figure-head of Maori Canoe.

he placed behind him, so as to conceal what he did. Then unfastening his waist-belt, he took from it some dried kumaras (sweet potatoes) which he placed in the bowl, and having mashed them into a pulp, he mixed them with water and handed the bowl to his hosts. When the Kahui Tipua tasted the sweetness of the mixture, they wanted more of it, and asked their guest where he got it from; he told them from across the sea. Soon after this, Tua-kaka-riki, one of their number, found a large totara tree on the beach, cast up by the sea. He measured its length, and found, after extending his arms along it ten times, that he had not reached the end of it. Delighted with his discovery, he hastened back to the pa. In the meantime, Rongo-i-tua reached the beach, and seeing the tree, mounted upon it, and made a mark near the butt end. When he, afterwards, heard Tua-kakariki claiming the tree by right of prior discovery, he told the people that it could not be claimed by Tua-kakariki, as it belonged to him long before in Hawaiki, from which place it had followed him; and that if they went and examined it, they would find his private mark upon it, made before leaving home. The discovery of the mark settled the question of ownership in favour of Rongo-i-tua. The tree was subsequently split in two, and out of each half a canoe was made; one called Manuka, the other Arai-te-Uru. Manuka was first finished, and the Kahui Tipua, impatient

to possess the kumara, sailed away to Hawaiki
in search of it. They obtained a cargo, and
returned; but, on planting them, they were
disappointed to find that none grew. In the
meantime, Rongo-i-tua sailed away on the same
errand in Arai-te-Uru. On reaching Whanga
ra (sunny cove), the place in Hawaiki where
the kumara grew, he ordered his men to
surround the chiefs house. They heard the
people inside repeating the kumara charms and
incantations. "Ah," said Rongo "those
karakias are what you need. Learn them."
After listening for a while, he and his men
acquired the knowledge they needed to ensure
the successful cultivation of the kumara.
Rongo-i-tua then sent his canoe back under
the command of Paki-hiwi-tahi and Hape-ki-
tauraki, as he intended to remain for some
time longer in Hawaiki. The voyage to New
Zealand was safely accomplished, and the cargo
partly discharged, when the canoe Arai-te-Uru
was caught in a storm and capsized off Moeraki,
the remains of the cargo being strewn along
the beach, where the petrified eel baskets and
calabashes and kumeras can still be seen at low
tide. When the time came for Rongo to return
he stepped in one day from Hawaiki to Ao-tea-
roa. The Kahui Tipua first saw a rainbow,
which suddenly assumed the form of a man,
and Rongo stood amongst them, hence he was
ever afterwards called Rongo tikei or Rongo
the "Strider."

TAMA-TEA-POKAI-WHENUA (Fair-Son—the circum-navigator), enjoys the credit of being the first to explore the coastline of this island, and to give names to the various places which he discovered. The promontory at the base of the On-Lookers was named KAI-KOURA by him because it was there he landed to cook crawfish. The chief object for which the voyage was undertaken by Tama was to discover the hiding place of his three wives who had deserted him. At the entrance of every inlet round the coast he waited and listened for any sound which might serve to indicate the whereabouts of the runaways. But it was not till he arrived off the mouth of the Arahura river that he heard voices; he immediately landed, but could not discover his wives, being unable to recognize them in the enchanted stones which strewed the bed of the river, and over which its waters murmuringly flowed. He did not know that the canoe, in which his wives escaped, had capsized at this spot, and that they and the crew had been changed into blocks of stone. Accompanied by his servant, he proceeded inland towards Mount Kaniere; on the way they stopped to cook some birds which they had killed. While preparing the meal the slave accidentally burnt his finger, which he thoughtlessly touched with the tip of his tongue; this act, as he was tapu, was an awful act of impiety, for which he was instantly punished by being transformed into a mountain, ever since known by his name, TUMŪ-AKI. Another consequence of his awful crime was that TAMATEA never found his wives, whose enchanted bodies furnish the Maori with the highly valued greenstone, the best kind of which is often spoilt by a flaw known as tutae koka, or the dung of the bird the slave was cooking when he licked his burnt finger.

The OGRE of the Molyneux (MATAU) was discovered and destroyed by TE RAPU-WAI, who were puzzled for a long time how to account for the mysterious disappearance of small parties of their people who went up into the hills bordering on the banks of the river to hunt for wekas. The mystery was cleared up by a woman, the sole survivor of one of these hunting parties, who succeeded in getting back to her home after some strange adventures. She told her friends that the party she was with were met on the hills by an Ogre who was accompanied by a pack of two headed-dogs. The giant killed all her companions and carried her off to his cave near the river where she lived with him; and in time became covered all over with scales from the Ogre's body. She was very miserable, and determined to escape; but the difficulty was how to accomplish her purpose, as the Ogre took care to fasten her by a cord which he kept jerking when ever she was out of his sight. As the cave was close to the river she crept to the entrance where raupo grew thickly, and having cut a quantity, tied it in bundles. The next day when the monster slept she crept out and formed the raupo bundles into a raft and tied the string by which she was held to some rushes which being elastic would yield when the cord was jerked and so prevent the immediate discovery of her flight. Getting on to the raft she dropped down the river, the swift current bearing her rapidly towards its mouth where her home was situated.

The Ogre did not wake for a long time, when he did he called out, " KAIAMIO. E ! where are you?" Not receiving an answer, he went to the entrance of the cave and searched ; but not finding any footprints there, he smelt the water, and at once discovered how she had escaped. Then in his rage he swallowed the river, and dried it up from end to end, but not before KAIAMIO was safely housed in her native village. After cleaning herself from the scales which covered her body, the woman told her people all she knew about the Ogre, and they resolved to put him to death. "When does he sleep?" they asked. "When the north-west wind blows," was her reply, "then he sleeps long and heavily." So they waited for the favourable wind, and then proceeded to the cave. Having collected a quantity of fern they piled it up at the entrance of the cave and then set fire to it. When the heat awoke the monster, he could think of no way of escape except through a hole in the roof; and while struggling to get through this, the people set upon him with clubs and beat him to death.

Chapter III.

FROM these fabulous legends we pass on to the shadowy traditions relating to tribes which have been utterly destroyed. Of these, the RAPU-WAI are said to have been the immediate successors of the KAHUI-TIPUA, they have left traces of their occupation in the shell-heaps found both along the coast and far inland. It was in their time that the country around Invercargill is said to have been submerged, the forests of Canterbury and Otago destroyed by fire, and the moa exterminated. I am inclined to think that Te Rapuwai and Waitaha were portions of the same tribe, Te Rapuwai forming the vanguard when the migration from the North Island took place. Several of my Maori authorities incline to this opinion, while others maintain that they were separate tribes, if so they were probably contemporaries, and like Rangitane and Ngai Tahu in subsequent times—one may have come from the west, and the other from the east coast of the North Island.

Of the WAITAHA very little is known, their traditions having almost entirely perished. But there is sufficient evidence to warrant the supposition that the few traditions which still remain were preserved by the remnant of Waitaha, who were spared by Ngatimamoe to work their fisheries and kumara plantations till they thought it necessary for their own safety to exterminate them in order to prevent their alliance with the invading Ngai Tahu. There is no reason therefore to regard the traditions relating to the Waitaha as mere fables,

It would appear that Waitaha—one of the original immigrants from Hawaiki—was the founder of the tribe. He came with Tama te Kapua and Nga toro i rangi in the canoe Arawa, and his taumata near Taupo is still pointed out. But at a very early date he or his immediate descendants must have left that locality, and travelled south. Separated by the stormy straits of Raukawa from their countrymen, Wa taha were long left in the enjoyment of peace and plenty, and as a consequence rapidly increased, till as the natives say " they covered the land like ants." The size of the pas, and the extent of the kitchen middens along the coast attributed to them, afford conclusive evidence as to their numbers. At Mairangi and Kapukariki (Cust) the remains of a walled pa extending for about three miles along the downs, existed till the settlement of Europeans in that locality. Many Maoris still living who used to go there annually to gather the stems of the cabbage-palm, — which grew luxuriantly on " soil enriched by the fat of man "—for making kauru, a favourite article of food—assert that twenty years ago, the broad outer ditch of the pah could be seen, and that from the bottom of it to the top of the bank was about seven feet, and that at regular intervals along the wall there were openings showing plainly where the gates had been. They recollected old men saying that these gates were known to have had names which were now forgotten. Tewai-Manongia and his son Tau hanga ahu are said to have ruled these pas at the time that they were destroyed by Ngatimamoe.

Some time before the Ngatimamoe invasion, about the year 1550 as near as we can guess, there lived on the banks of the Rakaia a chief named Tutewaimate, regarding whom a story worth recording has reached us. Moko, a robber chieftain, had fixed his stronghold on the Waipara, the choice of the spot being determined by the existence of a cave in close proximity to the highway, along which a regular trade was carried on up and down the coast; the preserved mutton-birds, dried fish, and kauru from the south being exchanged for preserved forest-birds, mats, etc., from the north. Moko was in the habit of robbing and murdering any small parties of carriers who might venture too near to him, and he might have continued to do so without molestation, as the carriers were for the most part slaves, whose death was not worth avenging, had he not been so unfortunate as to kill a near relation of the great Tutewaimate. This chief, already smarting under previous losses of property, was exasperated beyond all endurance by the murder of his kinsman, and summoned his tribe to destroy Moko and his band. The people responded in such numbers to his call, that when they started on their march, the dust they raised resembled the smoke of a great fire on the plains, and their spears darkened the sky. Leaving the bulk of his forces at Kapukariki, Tutewaimate pushed on early one morning with a few chosen warriors to Moko's stronghold. He found the place quite unprepared for an attack, all the men except Moko being away.

Having ascertained from some women whom he questioned that the robber chieftain was asleep in a cave hard by, he quietly approached the spot, where he found him lying asleep on a mat all unconscious of danger. But like a true knight he scorned to strike his sleeping foe, and raising his voice he uttered the following challenge:

"Tutewaimate	"I, Tutewaimate
Tutewaimate a Popotahi	Tutewaimate, son of Popotahi,
Te hau tuku mai i roto Rakaia	Swift as the wind from the Rakaia Gorge
Te mahea te hauku o te ata."	Have forestalled the drying of the morning dew."

The startled robber, raising himself to a sitting posture, replied:

"Ho, Moko	"Ho Moko,
Moko a Hautere	Moko, son of Hautere,
Te hau tuku mai runga maunga tere	The wind rushing down from Mt. Tere,
Te tangata i whangainga ki te mango mata."	The man fed upon uncooked shark."

As he uttered the last word the treacherous Moko, by a sudden and unexpected thurst, felled his generous foe to the ground, and soon put an end to his existence.

It is from the Waitaha that the following account of the destruction of a gigantic bird of prey has been handed down. The event occured in times preceding Tutewaimate and the period referred to in the scraps of Waitaha history which have survived. The story possesses peculiar interest when considered in connection with the discovery of the remains of the eagle *(Harpagornis moorei)* amongst the moa bones at Glenmark by Sir Julius Von Haast. A Pouakai (Old Glutton) had built its nest on a spur of Tawera (Mt. Torlesse) and darting down from thence it seized and carried off men, women, and, children, as food for itself and its young. For though its wings made a loud noise as it flew through the air, it rushed with such rapidity upon its prey that none could escape from its talons. At length a brave man called Te Hau o Tawera came on a visit to the neighbourhood, and finding that the people were being destroyed, and that they were so paralyzed with fear as to be incapable of adopting any means for their own protection, he volunteered to capture and kill this rapacious bird, provided they would do what he told them. This they willingly promised, and having procured a quanity of manuka saplings he went one night with fifty men to the foot of the hill, where there was a shallow pool, sixty feet in diameter. This he completely covered over with a network formed of saplings, and under this he placed the fifty men armed with spears and thrusting weapons, while he himself as soon as it was light, went out to lure the Pouakai from its nest. He did not go far before that "destroyer" spied him, and swooped down upon him. Hautere had now to run for his life, and just succeeded in reaching the shelter of the network when the bird pounced upon him, and in its violent efforts to reach its prey, forced its legs through the meshes, and becoming entangled, the fifty men plunged their spears into its body and after a desperate encounter succeeded in killing it.

The Waitaha after a peaceful occupation of what had then become known as the "food-abounding island," were obliged to resign possession of it into the hands of Ngatimamoe, and were ultimately destroyed or absorbed by them.

The origin of the NGATIMAMOE is nearly as obscure as that of their predecessors. Like them they came from the North Island, being probably driven down before a stronger tribe. Their pitiless treatment of Waitaha was afterwards repeated upon themselves by the stronger and more warlike Ngai Tahu. Their destruction of the Waitaha and their own subsequent destruction, accounts for the absence of all traditions relating to the visit of Abel

Tasman in 1642. Just as the destruction of the tribes inhabiting the shores of the straits by Rauparaha in this century, explains why no account of Captain Cook's visit in 1769 has been preserved amongst the natives now residing in that neighbourhood.

A genealogical table obtained from the natives at the extreme south of the island, traces their origin to the offspring of Awatopa. The following legend states the cause of their leaving the other island:—

Awatopa and Rauru were brothers, sons of Ruarangi and Manu tai hapu. They both commenced to build houses for themselves at the same time. Rauru was the first to finish; and having performed the ceremonies of purification, he announced his intention of going off on a voyage. His elder brother begged him to wait till he had completed his house, but this he refused to do, and, overcome with rage at his refusal, he killed him. The tribe hearing of what had taken place, avenged Rauru by killing Awatopa. This led to the secession of three families, children of the elder brother, namely— the Puhi kai ariki, Puhi manawanawa, and Matuku herekoti, who came south. The rest of the tribe remained behind. Relationship is claimed by the descendants of Ngatimamoe with Waikato through a Puhi of the Awatopa clan who settled there, and to Ngapuhi through Muru nui, who was connected with Maru kore, one of their ancestors.

During the Ngatimamoe occupation, an event occured which seems to throw some light upon the origin of the Chatham Islanders.

Tradition says that a canoe, manned entirely by chiefs whose names are forgotten, but who are known now as "Nga toko ono," or The Six, went out from Parakakariki to fish, and when a long way off from the shore a violent nor'west wind sprung up and drove them out to sea, and they were never heard of again. It is not at all improbable that this canoe reached the Chathams, and that the crew became the progenitors of one section of the present inhabitants. To Koti, a Maori Wesleyan minister who was stationed for some years on the principal island, states that the Morioris have preserved the names of many of the headlands around Akaroa, and that they number Mamoa (probably a corruption of Mamoe) amongst their ancestors. It is an interesting fact that many of the words in use by the Morioris are nearer akin to the Rarotongan form than the Maori equivalent.

It is quite clear that the Ngatimamoe, like the Ngai Tahu, came here from the east coast of the North Island. How long it was before their possession of this island was disputed, it is hard to guess correctly, but judging from their numbers, and the total subjugation of Waitaha to their rule when the Ngai Tahu appear on the scene, they could not have held possession of it for less than a hundred years.

Chapter IV.

THE reliable history of the Maori occupation of this island dates from A.D. 1650. About that time NGAI TAHU were located at HATAI-TAI near the entrance of WHANGA-NUI-ATARA, now called Wellington Harbour. The ancestors of this tribe came from Hawaiki in the canoes, TAKI-TIMU, KURA-HAU-PO, MATA-HORUA, and TAI-REA, and took possession of the Poverty Bay district in the North Island. The elopement of Tamatea's wives in the canoe, TAI-REA, and their subsequent pursuit by him brought to the knowledge of the Ngai Tahu, at a very early stage of their history, the existence of the island they called TUMUKI, and it was probably owing to the discovery of it that they began to move southwards, and finally resolved to become the possessors of it.

The Hataitai Pa was occupied by a band of warriors renowned for courage and daring, whose warlike propensities had made them rather obnoxious to their kinsmen and neighbours, the Ngatikahununu. Among this band dwelt an old chief named Kahukura te paku, who was connected with the Ngaitara tribe, then settled at Waimea, in the South Island. His son, Tu maro, was married to Rakai te kura, daughter of Tama ihu poro, the seventh from Tahu, the founder of the tribe. Shortly after the birth of their first child Tu Maro having reason to doubt the sincerity of his wife's attachment decided to separate from her. Without telling her what his intention was, he directed her to paint herself with red ochre, and to adorn her head with feathers, and to put on her best mats. When she had completed her toilet, he led her into the courtyard of a relative and left her there. On returning to his house he summoned all his immediate friends and relations, and informed them that it was his intention to leave HATAITAI immediately, as he could not live on friendly terms with those who had dishonoured him. His father approved of the proposed step, and acting on his advice their hapu, carrying with them their families and all their movable goods, crossed the straits and entered Blind Bay, along the coast of which they sailed till they reached the mouth of the Waimea River, where they landed and built a pa. Here, for upwards of twenty years the Ngaitara, Ngatiwhata, and Ngatirua, sub-sections of the Ngai Tahu tribe, separated from their main body at Hataitai, grew into such importance through their alliance with Ngatimamoe, that they came at last to be regarded more in the light of independent tribes than parts of one and the same ; and this often complicates the narrative.

But what serves to complicate still further the history of this period was the existence of small settlements in the sounds of natives from the west coast of the North Island including detachments of Rangitane, Ngatihauwa, Ngatihape, Ngai te he iwi, Ngai tawake, Ngati whare puka, and Ngai tu rahui. The Rangitane appear to have been the most important. Te Hau was their chief, and his cultivations at Te Karaka, known as Kapara te hau and O kainga, are still pointed out. Kupe, the great navigator is said to have poured salt-water upon these cultivations for the purpose of destroying them, and so formed pools which remain to this day (?). These natives never seem to have extended their settlements much beyond the sounds, and little of their history worth recording has been preserved by the remnant of their descendants who escaped destruction at the hands of Te Rauparaha.

Beyond Waimea, the Ngatiwairangi and Ngatikopiha, who in common with Ngatimamoe and Ngai Tahu were descended from Tura, took up their abode and spread from there all down the west coast.

About twenty-five years after the secession of Kahukura te paku and his followers, communication with Hataitai was re-opened under the following circumstances. Tuahuriri, deserted in infancy by Tu maro, had now attained to man's estate, and had settled with his wives on the south-east coast of the North Island. But

he could not rest till he had solved a question
which had troubled him all his life. Once
when a child he had been startled by hearing
the mother of one of his playmates, whom he
had struck, exclaim, "What a bullying fellow
this bastard is." Running up to his own mother,
he immediately asked if it was true that he was a
bastard. "No," she said. "Then where," he
asked, "is my father?" "Look where the
sun sets, that is where your father dwells."
He kept these words treasured up in his
memory; and now, having attained to man's
estate, he determined to go in search of his
father. Leaving his wives behind him he
embarked with seventy men in a war canoe,
and crossed the straits to Waimea; arrived
there, he landed and drew up the canoe in front
of the pa. The inhabitants came forth to
welcome him, and invited him to occupy the
residence of their chief. On entering the house
Tuahuriri laid himself down on his back near
the door, whilst his companions seated themselves round the sides of the house. As no
one in the place recognised any of them, the
usual preparations were made for their
destruction; as it was always held by Maoris
that those who were not known friends must
be regarded as enemies, and treated accordingly.
Kahukura te paku stationed armed men all
round the house; and while he was preparing
to attack the new comers, the women and slaves
were busy heating the stones and preparing the

ovens to cook their bodies in. While these preparations were being made, and everyone was longing for the time when the bodies would be cooked and ready for them to feast upon, the children of the village came flocking round the entrance curious to see the strangers. One more venturesome than the rest climbed up to the window, and communicated to those behind him what he saw; while so occupied, Tuahuriri, looking up at the roof, said, "Ah, just like the red battens of my grandfather Kahukura te paku's house which he left over the other side at Kauwhakaarawaru." The boy on hearing this ran and told the men who were lying in wait. They made him repeat the words several times, and then Kahukura te paku said, I never left any house or painted battens on the other side, only the boy on whose account we came across. Go and ask him his name." Then one arose and approached, and called out, "Inside there. Eh! Sit up. Tell me who you are!" Then Tuahuriri sat up and said, "I am Te hiku tawatawa o te raki" (the name given to him by his father when he was born). The man went back and told Kahukura te paku, who was overwhelmed with shame when he discovered that he had been craving after the flesh of his own grandson. Approaching the house he told him to come forth, not by the door, but the window, so that they might take the tapu off the wood and stones which they had got ready o cook him and his friends with, as the intention had defiled them. Having clambered through the window and embraced his grandfather, Tuahuriri felt that he was safe; nevertheless he did not forget the indignity to which he had been subjected by his own relations, and he determined to take the first opportunity of punishing them for it. When returning to his own home with Kahukura te paku a few weeks afterwards, the people of Waimea begged Tuahuriri to come back and visit them in the autumn, when food would be plentiful, and they could entertain him more hospitably. But instead of doing so, he waited till he knew that they had planted their fields, and had nothing in their storehouses, then, taking one hundred men in addition to the seventy who went with him before, he re-crossed the straits. When he landed with all his followers the inhabitants of Waimea welcomed him very warmly, but apologised for the smallness of the quantity of food which they set before him, which, they assured him, was owing, not to inhospitality, but to the emptiness of their stores. When every particle of food in the place was consumed Tuahuriri returned home. Shortly after his departure the house he occupied was accidentally burnt down; the site of it was soon covered with a luxuriant crop of wild cabbage, which the inhabitants of the pa were driven by hunger to gather and eat, and in consequence of their doing so they all died in great pain. The fatal effects which followed their feasting on greens were attributed by the Maoris to the agency of the atuas of their chiefs, who resented the indignity offered to them by those who dared to eat what had grown on ground rendered "tapu" by contact with their sacred persons.

The chief, Tuahuriri had from some cause incurred the ill-will of a powerful member of his own tribe, the veteran warrior Hika oro roa, who assembled his relations and dependents, and led them to the attack of Tuahuriri's pa, situated somewhere on the east coast of the North Island. They reached the fortress at dawn of day; and as the leader was preparing to take the foremost place in the assault, a youth named Turuki, eager to distinguish himself, rushed past Hika oro roa, who uttered an exclamation of surprise and indignation, asking, in sneering tones, "Why a nameless warrior should dare to try and snatch the credit of a victory he had done nothing to win?" Turuki, burning with shame at the taunt, rushed back to the rear and addressed himself to Tutekawa, who was the head of his family, and besought him to withdraw his contingent and attack the pa himself from the opposite side, and for ever prevent such a reproach from being uttered again. Tutekawa, who felt the insult as keenly as his young relative, instantly adopted his suggestion; and so rapidly did he effect the movement, that his absence was not discovered before he had successfully assaulted the pa and his name was being shouted forth as the victor. Tuahuriri was surprised asleep in his whare, but succeeded in escaping, leaving his two wives, Hine kai taki and Tuara whati, to their fate. These women were persons of great distinction, and were related to all the principal families in that

part of the country, and their lives ought to
have been quite safe in the hands of their
husband's relations. But Tutekawa, who was
a man of cruel disposition, finding the husband
had escaped, killed both the women. As the
war party were re-embarking a few hours after,
Tuahuriri came out to the edge of the forest,
which reached nearly to the shore, and calling
Tutekawa, asked him if he had got his waist-
cloth, belt, and weapons; on being answered in
the affirmative, he begged that they might be
given back to him. Tutekawa then stepped
forward and flung them towards him. After
picking them up, Tuahuriri threatened his
cousin with the vengeance of his atuas for the
injury he had done to him; and retiring into
the depths of the forest, he invoked the help of
his familiar spirits, and by their agency raised
the furious gale known as Hau o Rongomai.
This tempest dispersed Hika oro roa's fleet, and
and many of his canoes were upset and the crews
drowned. Tutekawa with much difficulty
reached the South Island, where, to escape the
vengeance of Tuahuriri, he decided to remain.
He had nothing to fear from the Ngatimamoe,
to whom he was related on the mother's side,
and he knew that his presence would be
welcome to them, because he was willing to
turn his arms against the remnant of Waitaha
who still maintained their independence. We
now take leave of Tutekawa for some years,
and return to trace the fortunes of the warriors

at Hataitai, of whom we have heard nothing since Tu maro's secession.

Though constantly at war with their neighbours or quarrelling amongst themselves, they had succeeded hitherto in maintaining their ground; but certain events occurred after the fall of Te mata ki kai poika and the defeat of Tuahuriri, which ultimately led to their migration to the South Island.

The first was the marriage of Tiotio's two daughters to Te Hautaki, which was brought about in the following manner:—Te Hautaki, who was the chief of a hapu living at Kahu, and allied to Ngatimamoe, was one day driven out to sea from the fishing ground by a gale of wind. Fearing that his canoe would be upset, and being unable to get back to his own place, he tried to reach the opposite shore of the straits, and with much difficulty effected a landing after dusk at Whanga nui a tara, just below the NGAITAHU pa. "We are all dead men," he said to his crew, "unless we can reach the house of Tiotio unobserved." Tiotio was the upoko ariki, or hereditary high priest of the tribe, and probably Hautaki regarded him in the light of a connection, since his son Tuteuretira was married to a Ngatimamoe woman and living amongst that tribe. "Is there any one of you," he asked, "who can point out this chief's house?" Fortunately one of the crew had been before to Hataitai and was able to act as guide. Having drawn up their canoe, they all marched noiselessly in single file till they reached the remotest of the chief's houses, which were distinguished from others around them by their great height and size. Passing by those of Maru, Manawa, and Rakai tauwheke, they came to that of Tiotio. Entering the house, they found his wife seated beside a fire near the door, and the old man himself lying down at the farthest end. Roused by the noise of their footsteps, the old chief stood up and asked who they were, Te Hautaki replied, " It is I." No sooner were they aware who it really was than the old wife set up a cry of welcome ; but she was instantly checked by her husband, who dreaded the consequence of rousing the pa, and begged her not to attract attention, as that would endanger the lives of the whole party. He then told her to set food quickly before them, as they could not be killed after having been entertained as guests by the chief tohunga of the tribe. In obedience to his wishes, she placed a *poha of preserved koko before them ; and when they had finished their meal, she went over with a message from her husband to Rakai tauwheke, who was married to two of their daughters, Tahupare and Rongopare. That chief, on hearing of Te Hautaki's arrival, asked whether he had been allowed to eat in his father-in-law's house ; on being answered in the affirmative, " That is enough," he said, " I will come and see him in the morning." Before doing so however, he sent to inform Manawa and Maru and others ;

* Vessel made of kelp filled with preserved birds.

and as soon as what had happened became generally known throughout the pa, the warriors assembled round Tiotio's house, and with yells and frantic cries hurled their spears against the roof and sides, and behaved as if they intended to pull the house down. When old Tiotio remonstrated with them, they ceased their violence, and invited Te Hautaki to come out to them, when there was much talking and speech-making of a friendly kind, which finally ended in a proposal that Tiotio's remaining daughters—Rakai te kura and Mahanga taki— should be given in marriage to Te Hautaki. As all the parties concerned were agreeable to this, the marriage took place without any delay. The Ngai Tahu chiefs asked many questions of their visitor about his surroundings in the other island, and they were so favourably impressed with his answers, that many responded to his invitation to accompany him when he returned. The final migration, however, did not take place till some time after Te Hautaki's return.

What caused the step to be taken was this: Tapu a Kahununu chief heard those who had seen Rakai tauwheke's house at Hataitai praising the workmanship of it, and, being jealous, said — "What is his house to my *Kopapa, which will carry me along the backbone of Rongo rongo." These words coming to RAKAI TAUWHEKE'S ears, were interpreted by him to mean a curse, and when Tapu afterwards

---

* "Kopapa," little canoe. "Rongo rongo," renown.

came on a visit with some friends to Hataitai, RAKAI TAUWEKE fell upon him and killed him, but spared all his companions, whom he allowed to return safely home. But dreading the vengeance of Tapu's tribe, the Ngai Tahu abandoned Hataitai, and crossed over the Straits in a body to Moioio, an island in one of the Sounds close to Kai hinu, where there was a mixed settlement of Ngaitara and Ngatimamoe. Here they lived peaceably with their neighbours for some time till their anger was aroused by the discovery that they had joined in eating the body of a Ngai Tahu man which they had found in the forest, where, unknown to his friends he had died. This was considered a very gross insult, and was avenged in the following manner :—Someone was sent to fetch the leg and thigh-bones of AO MARERE, a Ngaitara chief, whose remains had been lately discovered in a cave by some Ngai Tahu women when gathering flax on the slopes of Kaihinu. Out of these bones hooks were made, and when Ngaitara went out to fish a Ngai Tahu man, taking one of the hooks, went with them; and when the fish greedily attacked the bait, and were drawn up to the surface in rapid succession, he said, in a tone to be heard and remarked, "Ha! Ha! How the old man buried up there nips." The words were noted, and it was agreed that they could only refer to the desecration of their chief's grave, and to set the question at rest a person was sent to examine it, when it was found that part of the skeleton had been removed. As the Ngaitara did not regard this as a justifiable act of retaliation for their having eaten the body which they found, they determined to avenge it. An opportunity of doing so was afforded to them shortly afterwards, when a party of Ngai Tahu women came as usual to the neighbourhood of Kai hinu to gather flax. While they were busily employed at their work, the Ngaitara attacked and killed the whole of them, amongst whom was the daughter of PURAHO. This chief mourned sorely for his child and vowed to avenge her; but before he could do so, he was himself killed by the same people, who, feeling that they had incurred the vengeance of Ngai Tahu, were resolved to follow up what they had done and to be the first in the field. Observing from the mainland, which was only a short way off, that Puraho and Manawa went every morning at dawn to a particular spot outside the pa, it was arranged to plant an ambush there for them. Accordingly, during the night, two warriors were sent to secrete themselves in the neighbourhood, who succeeded in killing one of the chiefs.

The death of Puraho convinced Ngai Tahu of the insecurity of their position at Moioio, and they determined to abandon it and to remove to O te Kaue, at the mouth of the Wairau river, where they built a strongly fortified pa. As soon as they had provided for the safety of their families, they began to take measures for avenging the death of Puraho, and the women so mercilessly slaughtered by Ngaitara.

They first attacked a neighbouring pa, and captured it. Amongst the prisoners was the chief RAPA A TE KURI, who was brought by his captors to Maru, in order that he might have the satisfaction of putting him to death as utu for his father and sister. But, contrary to their expectations, and to the annoyance and disgust of everyone, Maru spared the prisoner's life. Waitai was so exasperated by his culpable leniency, that he immediately withdrew with three hundred followers, and sailed away to the south, settling for a time at Pukekura (Taiaroa Head). On taking his departure he warned those who remained against a leader who would encourage them to attack his enemies and then deprive them of their right to put their captives to death. "I will never again join with Maru," he said, "but will fight my enemies where I shall not be interfered with." Though considerably weakened by the secession of Waitai, Ngai Tahu wished to continue the war, but were opposed by Maru, who, being related to Ngaitara, did not like to see them crushed.

While the Ngai Tahu chiefs were disputing about their future plans, Te Kaue and Tau hiku went out one day to fish, in order to silence the cries of their grandchildren for a change of food. They had not gone far from the shore when both canoes were enveloped in a fog; the crews could hear the splashing of the paddles, but could not see each other; they succeeded, however, in reaching the fishing ground, and Tau hiku was the first to drop his anchor, and just as Te Kaue was about to do the same, he became aware that they were being pursued, and that the sound of paddling proceeded from canoes sent after them by Ngatimamoe. Te Kaue turned at once and pulled towards the shore, but Tau hiku was surrounded and taken prisoner. A running fight was then maintained between Te Kaue's canoe and Ngatimamoe. The fog prevented the position of affairs being seen from the shore, where Ngai Tahu were in complete ignorance of the danger their friends were in, though, as the canoes approached the land, sounds of strife reached their ears.

Te Kaue managed to keep the enemy from coming to close quarters by the help of his nephew, who, acting upon his instructions, watched his opportunity whenever they came close enough to seize the man nearest to him, jerk him on board his own canoe, and kill him by cleaving open his skull; and as his blood spirted out over his comrades, they drew back with horror, and gave Te Kaue a slight advantage in the race. This was repeated again and again till they got quite close to the shore, when the fog rose and discovered the combatants to the people of the pa, who were wondering what it could be that was causing such a din. Manawa and others ran down to the landing place, where they saw Tau hiku, their tohunga, lying bound in the bottom of the Ngatimamoe canoe, which had pursued Te Kaue to within a few yards of the beach. The Ngai Tahu were overwhelmed with grief and alarm, and wailed forth their last farewell to the old priest doomed to fill the enemy's oven; in acknowledgment of their parting cries, he held up two fingers.

Ngai Tahu were paralyzed by the loss of their wisest tohunga, for there was no one to take his place—no one who could read the omens and tell the propitious time for attacking their enemies, or forewarn them of approaching danger. The chiefs assembled and continued long in anxious consultation. "Have we no one," they asked, "of the race of Tau hiku who can enlighten us—one with whom he has left his knowledge?" They called his daughter and questioned her. She advised them to summon Tau hiku's son Pohatu, but they ridiculed the idea; he had never displayed any talent, and had from boyhood consorted with slaves in preference to persons of his own rank. "Can such a one as Pohatu enlighten and direct us? His place is in the kitchen beside the cooking fire; what can the defiled know about sacred things!" Still his sister urged that he might be sent for and questioned; so at last they took Pohatu, and, having stripped him of his clothes, they took him to the water and cleansed him, and then

WAR CANOES.

performed certain incantations over him to consecrate him and make him "tapu." When the ceremonies were completed they asked him what Tau hiku meant by holding up two fingers. "Two years," he replied. "You must wait for that time before you attempt to avenge his death, in order that the grass may hide the oven in which he was cooked."

During this period of forced inaction, the Ngai Tahu were particularly anxious to know what their enemies were doing, and in this they were greatly assisted by a man named Kiti, who was related to both tribes, and who by common consent acted as spy for both. Kiti alarmed the Ngai Tahu with the reports he brought to them of the formidable preparations being made by Ngatimamoe for the coming struggle. Besides the ordinary weapons, they had prepared spears pointed with the barbed and poisonous sting of the ray—of which everyone appeared to stand in great dread. As the time approached for commencing hostilities, all hearts were filled with alarm, and as this feeling of dread increased the older chiefs felt that something must be done to counteract it, or their defeat and destruction were certain. They decided, therefore, to take the initiative, and to commence hostilities at once. Then Maru rose and called upon the veteran warriors, the heroes of former battles, to recount the story of their deeds so as to inspire the tribe with courage: — "Rise up, Te Kaue, and tell the people what

thou achieved at Whanga nui a tara!" But Te
Kaue kept his seat, and replied:—"Ah! that
was accomplished in the midst of thousands
supporting me, but here, single-handed, what
can I do!" Turning to another, he said:—
"Rise up, O Manawa, and tell the story of thy
brave deeds at Waihao!" But Manawa only
repeated Te Kaue's words:—"They were done
amidst supporting thousands." One after
another the heroes were appealed to, but all in
vain; till Maru turned to Rakai tauwheke:—
"Rise, O Wheke!" "Yes," he said, "I will;
since all these brave men decline, I will force
the way—I will charge the foe—I will lead the
people on to victory! Rouse thyself, Pohatu!
Rouse thyself, O seer! Dig the wells, rear the
mounds that you may see how the tatare (dog-
fish) of Tane moehau (his mother) will burst
the nets!"

The bold bearing of Rakai tauwheke revived
the drooping spirits of his tribe. His words
inspired them with courage; and the omens
given by Pohatu decided Ngai Tahu to attack
the enemy at once. They swarmed up the hill-
side that separated them from the pa; but
Ngatimamoe, thanks to Kiti, were well informed
of their movements, and before they could reach
the top, came pouring over the ridge, filling the
air with their yells of defiance, and raining down
their dreaded spears upon the advancing ranks.
Rakai tauwheke kept well in front, and succeeded
in warding off every weapon aimed against him,

and finally reached the top of the hill, where he was soon joined by others, and there, by a prodigious display of valour, he completely routed the enemy, who broke and fled in every direction. Tu te uretira pursued after Tu ma taiao, a Ngatimamoe chief married to a sister of Maru, and would have caught him but for an accident to his foot, which obliged him to give up the chase. As he did so he called out to his flying foe:—"It is only this painful foot which prevents my overtaking you." To which the other sneeringly replied:—"Are you the one who can catch by morning the moving feet, swift as the raupo swaying in the wind?" "Ah!" said Tu te uretira, "Can you escape by morning the cutting toetoe of Turau moa?" No vain boast, as he afterwards proved.

Among those who fell upon this occasion was Kana te pu, who had sadly misread the omens. In his island home at *Rakiura he dreamt that he caught a white crane, which kicked him in the chest while vainly struggling to get free. Interpreting this dream to mean that he was destined to overcome some famous Ngai Tahu warrior, he went to a neighbouring stream to bind the omen, and then eager to distinguish himself summoned his followers and took his departure for the seat of war. In the crisis of the battle when Rakai tauwheke was slaying those to the right and left of him with his taiaha, Kana te pu, watching his opportunity, sprang

* Stewarts Island.

upon his shoulders, and held him so firmly that
he could not draw his arms back again. He
tried in vain to shake him off, but by a sudden
movement of his hands he jerked the point of
his weapon against the head of his opponent,
and then, by a violent contortion of the body,
succeeded in inflicting a mortal wound, and the
"white crane" fell dead at his feet.

After the defeat of Ngatimamoe at Tete
Whai, or battle of the ray-barbed spears, peace
was restored for some years, and Ngai Tahu
were permanently settled at Wairau.

But trouble was brewing for Ngatimamoe in
a quarter whence it was least expected.

For many years two Ngai Tahu chiefs had
lived amongst them, and having married their
women were regarded as being thoroughly
identified with them. One appears to have
been of a moody sullen disposition whilst the
other was quite the reverse, and made himself
so popular that he was elected chief of the hapu
with whom he lived. Apoka lived a solitary
life with his two wives and a few slaves, while
Tu te uretira ruled a pa containing three
hundred Ngatimamoe. Apoka's ground was
too poor to cultivate and game rarely frequented
the woods in his neighbourhood. He was
forced to depend for subsistence on fern root.
He bore his privations cheerfully till his
suspicions were aroused that his wives partook
of better fare than they chose to set before him.
He daily noticed that their breath gave evidence

of their having eaten some savoury food. He remarked that although they paid frequent visits to their relatives who resided at a place celebrated for the variety and plenty of its supplies, they never brought anything to vary the sameness of his diet. He was convinced these visits were made to replenish secret stores concealed from him by his wives at the suggestion of their own people, who perhaps thought that if he once tasted the good things of Waipapa he might advise his tribe to take possession of it by force. His wives when questioned indignantly denied that they ate anything better than the food given to their lord. Convinced, however, that they deceived him, and brooding over his wrong, he resolved to seek his cousin's advice. On drawing near the settlement he found Tu te uretira in the midst of a large kumera plantation urging on the labours of a hundred men, who asked his cousin whether he should cause the men to desist from their work and adjourn to the pa to listen to whatever he might have to say. "No," replied Apoka, "my business is with you alone, let the men continue their work." The two then visited the *"tuahu," where they performed certain rites, and then retired to the verandah of the chief's house, where one of his wives had arranged some food for the refreshment of the visitor. Tu te uretira blessed the

---

* Small enclosure where offerings to the Atuas were placed, and prayers offered up.

food, and then invited his cousin to partake of it, begging him to refresh himself, and then tell him his business before the people returned from the field to prepare a feast in his honour. Apoka bent his head a long time in silence, and then said, "I am stupefied, I am amazed at the variety of food;" then pointing to each basket before him in succession he asked what they contained. He then resumed his silent attitude, and fixing his eyes on the ground remained in that position for some hours. He was roused from his reverie by the arrival of the tribe bringing the feast they had prepared, and which they set down in little piles before him. He made the same answer to all their pressing invitations to eat, "I am overcome, I am astonished, I cannot eat." "But how is it," enquired his cousin, "that you who married Ngatimamoe women should express such astonishment at the every-day fare of that people, surely you enjoy the same advantages as myself by your connection with them?" In reply Apoka told him his suspicions respecting his wives, which had received confirmation by what he had seen during this visit. Tu te uretira advised him to refer the matter to the elders of the tribe at Wairau who would be only too glad to take up his quarrel in order that they might dispossess Ngatimamoe of Waipapa. Apoka, satisfied with the advice, rose and returned fasting to his home, where his wives brought him the usual meal, of which he partook, and then retired to rest.

To lull any suspicions that might arise respecting the object of his visit to Wairau, he set off for Waipapa early the next morning accompanied by a slave bearing his fishing tackle. The canoes were already launched when he arrived, and all the men were about starting on a fishing expedition. On seeing him, however, the principal chief of the place gave immediate orders that the canoes should be drawn up, and that everyone should return to the pa out of respect to his son-in-law. But when Apoka assured him that his only object in coming was to go with them to fish, and that he would be disappointed unless they went, the canoes were manned and they all started for the fishing ground. Only two fishes were caught, and these by Te Apoka. The whole party were much annoyed at their want of success, and regarded it as an ill omen. On landing, his friends begged Apoka to remain and partake of their hospitality, but he refused to stay and ordered his servant to bring the fish and to follow him. The first thing he did when he got home was to hang the fish up on the "tuahu" as an offering to his atua. He then ordered his wives to prepare a quantity of fern-root as he intended to take a long journey.

When his arrangements were completed, he took one fish, and fastening it to the end of a rod, bore it on his shoulder to Wairau. His tribe no sooner saw him than they recognised the symbol which indicated a troubled mind, and immediately guessed his errand. They gave him a hearty welcome, and crowded eagerly round to hear the story of his wrongs. As he detailed the various circumstances their indignation rose higher and higher; and when he proposed to lead them against the Ngatimamoe, young and old shouted with delight. It was agreed that the close relationship existing between himself and his wives shielded them from punishment, but that the insult they had offered must be wiped out by the blood of their tribe. Fearing to go near Tu te uretira lest the enemy should be warned, they took a very circuitous route and came upon the doomed pa at dawn. Apoka, knowing it was the custom of the place to go early every day to fish, placed his men in ambush round the pa; directing Uhikore, a warrior famed for his bravery, to lie in wait under the principal chief's canoe. His arrangements were scarcely completed before Paua himself appeared. He was a very tall man, and so powerful that, unaided, he could launch a war canoe. He placed his shoulder against the stern of his canoe to push it as usual into the water, when Uhikore rose and felled him to the ground. The cry that Paua was killed struck terror into the hearts of the Ngatimamoe, and ere they could recover themselves the place was stormed and taken. A few only escaped; the rest were either eaten or reduced to slavery.*

* Fall of Waipapa is placed by some before the battle of Ika a whaturoa.

Apoka, whose hatred seemed implacable, resolved to destroy that portion of Ngatimamoe over whom Tu te uretira ruled. He sent Uhikore clothed in the spoils of Paua to inform him of his design. As he approached, the garments which he wore were recognised by Paua's relations, who bewailed his sad fate with loud lamentations. Deserted by Tu te uretira, who returned with Uhikore to the camp of his victorious countrymen, and dreading an attack, the Ngatimamoe abandoned their settlements, and fled down the coast towards Kaikoura, where they remained undisturbed for some years. Having chosen a strong position at Peketa, on the hill-side at the mouth of the Kahutara, they built a fortified pa; and being joined by other sections of the tribe, they were emboldened to attack a fishing party of the Ngai Tahu. They succeeded in capturing all the canoes but one, that of Te Kaue, which escaped with the loss of the most of the crew. This led to a renewal of hostilities between the two tribes: a battle was fought at Opokihi, and again on the banks of the Kahutara, in both which engagements Ngatimamoe were defeated. They then retired within their fortifications, and Ngai Tahu laid siege, but failed for many months to effect an entrance.

A council of chiefs was then held, at which Rakai tauwheke proposed to draw the enemy out by stratagem. His plan was approved of, and he proposed to carry it out on the following morning. Putting on two feather mats, and armed with a patu paraoa, he went before dawn to the beach, and entering the surf threw himself down and allowed the waves to carry him backwards and forwards, occasionally raising his arm a little that it might appear like a fin. The sentinels soon took notice of the dark object in the water, which they concluded must be either a seal or a young whale. The cry of "He ika moana! he ika moana!" brought the whole pa to their doors, and a general rush towards the beach followed, each striving to secure the prize. The pa was so close to the shore that the people did not hesitate to open the gates, and the foremost man plunged into the surf; but before he could discover his mistake, the supposed fish rose and struck him dead. The alarm was immediately given, and the crowd fell back within the stockade and the scheme failed. Weakened and wearied by the war, the two tribes laid down their arms and made peace, which continued till broken by Manawa's raid on Omihi.

The Ngatimamoe at that place were partly ruled by Tukiauau, a Ngai Tahu and nephew of Te Rangi whakaputa, who was related to the former tribe on the mother's side. For some reason Manawa attacked these people. Having approached the pa with six companions for the purpose of reconnoitring, he caught sight of the "tu ao kura," or head ornament of Rakaimomona, father of Tukiauau, who was

sitting outside his house. Manawa hurled a
spear in that direction and pierced the old man
through the heart ; then without being aware
of what he had done, he returned to join the
main body of his followers, resolving to attack
the pa at dawn. Within the pa all was
confusion, the death of Rakaimomona produced
a panic, and it was decided to evacuate the
place during the night ; but in order to conceal
their intentions from the enemy, they left fires
burning in every house. Manawa, ignorant of
what had happened, cautiously approached at
dawn to invest the place ; but not seeing anyone
moving about, he sent scouts to the top of a
neighbouring hill from which the pa could be
overlooked, and they soon returned with the
intelligence that the place was deserted.
Manawa immediately returned to Waipapa and
reported what had happened to Maru, who
offered to follow the fugitives and to bring
them back ; *his secret reason for doing this
being that his Ngatimamoe connections might
have an opportunity of avenging Rakaimomona's
death at some future time.* He found Tukiauau
at Tutae putaputa, where he was preserving his
father's head, which he intended to keep,
according to custom, at one end of his house,
where, surrounded by mats, he and his children
could look upon it, and think the old man was
still amongst them. Maru urged Tukiauau not
to go any further, but to build his pa where he
was, at Pakihi. This he consented to do, and

Maru returned home. Not long afterwards a circumstance occurred which indicates the existence of such a curious state of things, that it is hard to understand how any tribe could exist when subject to such internal disorders, and where its leading members were animated by such opposite motives.

Maru's daughter Rakai te kura was betrothed in infancy to Te Rangi tauhunga, son of Te Rangi whakaputa; notwithstanding this, she married with her father's consent Tu a keka; this so incensed Te Rangi whakaputa that, on hearing of it, he went straight to Maru's enclosure and killed one of his servants, Tu manawa rua, right before his face. So gross an outrage could not be patiently borne, and Maru sought the protection of Tukiauau with whom he remained till Te Rangi whakaputa was forced by the Ngai Tahu, who regretted the absence of a favourite chief, to go and ask him to come back. On his arrival at Pakihi Maru presented him with a large poha or kelp-vessel full of preserved birds, which was called Tohu raumati. Te Rangi whakaputa, while accepting it, refused to allow it to be opened, saying, "It shall be for you Maru when you return to us." As soon as Maru did reach Waipapa he proposed that the poha should be eaten on the war path, as they had a death to avenge. Maru could not kill the man who insulted him nor any of his people, but he hoped that in fighting the common enemy some of Te Rangi whakaputa's kin would be killed, and so payment for his murdered servant and injured honour would be obtained. Ngai Tahu, always eager for war, responded to his invitation and followed him to the attack of Kura te au, a pa belonging to Ngaitara. It was taken, and amongst the prisoners was Hine Maka, a woman of rank, who was brought to Maru in order that he might put her to death; but instead of doing so he gave her in marriage to his son, and when asked the reason for this strange act his reply was, "When my descendants, the offspring of this marriage, are taunted with being slaves on the mother's side, the particulars will be enquired into, and then it will be found that the mother was taken prisoner when the death of my father was being avenged, so that the memory of my father's death having been avenged will be better preserved by sparing this woman than by killing her."

It was about this time that Ngai Tahu had a visit from a celebrated Ngatimamoe chief Te Rangitauneke, who lived at Ohou near the Opihi River. He came as the champion of his tribe for the purpose of challenging Manawa to single combat with spears. But Manawa's friends would not allow him to accept the challenge, fearing that he might be killed. Maru, however, was allowed to take it up, and at the appointed time, in the presence of the assembled warriors, the two chiefs encountered each other. Rangitauneke was the first to hurl his spear, which Maru parried; then Maru not wishing to kill him, threw his spear in such a manner as to pass between his legs and through his apron. Te Rangitauneke acknowledged himself beaten and returned home. Shortly afterwards it was reported that he was killed at Upokopipi, having been surprised by his enemies while sleeping in the grass outside his pa. His atua Matamata, however, came to his rescue and licked up his blood, when he recovered and re-entered the pa, which during his temporary absence had fallen into his enemies' hands ; having routed them he set fire to the place, and retired with his friends towards the south, where, after many encounters with Ngai Tahu, he eventually died at Waihopai.

During the peace which followed the taking of Kura te au, the most friendly intercourse existed between the various Maori communities ; to such an extent did this prevail that Manawa even ventured to visit Tukiauau, whose father he had killed a few years before. The object of the visit was to see the far-famed beauty Te ahua rangi, daughter of Tu whakapau, with a view to making at some future time a proposal of marriage on behalf of his son Te rua hikihiki. He did not conceal from his own people that he hoped, by means of this marriage, to secure the Ngatimamoe hapu, to which the beauty belonged, as his son's serfs. The idea tickled the fancy of his followers, who, while employed fastening the side-boards of his canoe preparatory to his departure, could not refrain from joking about the people who were so soon to become their chief's "pori." "Eh! this is a grand idea," said one. "Ah!" said another, "wait till you have successfully snared the thick-necked bird of Hika roroa."

The visit passed off pleasantly, and Manawa was returning home; the people were flocking to the beach side of the pa to wish him good-bye, when Te Rangi whakaputa hearing some one sobbing, turned round and saw it was Tukiauau. "Are you a woman that you cry?" "No," said he, "I am only grieving at my brother's departure." "Beware!" was the reply. "Do not use green flax, but scraped flax. Do not take the foremost nor the hindermost, but the one in the middle, Kopu para para, the star of the year himself. Do not divulge this hint of mine." The suggestion, so treacherously made by Manawa's friend and companion in arms, was not forgotten, as the sequel will show. Having waited an appropriate time, Manawa returned to Pakihi to obtain the formal consent of Tu whakapau to his daughter's marriage with his son. Accompanied by one hundred followers he approached the pa, being welcomed with the customary greetings. Amongst his party were Maru's brother and several other relations of his; these were led by Hine umutahi to her house, while the rest were shown into a large house set apart for their reception. Manawa was the last to enter the pa, and as he bent his head in passing through the low gate-way, Tukiauau, who was standing just inside it,

MAORI LADIES.

struck him a violent blow with a stone axe.
Manawa staggered forward, but before he
reached his companions he received a still more
violent blow on the head. Immediately he got
into the house the door was closed, and the old
chief, after wiping the blood from his face,
addressed his men. He told them that their
case was hopeless. Caught in a trap and
surrounded by overpowering numbers they
must prepare to die; all that he desired was
that an attempt should be made to convey to
the Ngai Tahu tidings of their cruel fate.
Many volunteered for the dangerous service.
One having been chosen from the number,
Manawa, after smearing his forehead with the
blood from his own wound, charged him to be
brave, and commiting him to the care of his
atuas sent him forth. Hundreds of spears were
aimed at the messenger, who fell transfixed
before he had advanced a pace. Again and
again the attempt to escape was repeated, but
in vain. The imprisoned band grew dispirited,
and Manawa failed to obtain a ready response
to his call for more volunteers. At length a
youth closely related to him offered to make a
last attempt. The moment was propitious; the
enemy, certain of success, guarded the door
with less vigilance. Smeared with the dying
chief's blood, and charged with his last message
to his family and tribe, Tahua sprang forth;
warding off the spears hurled at him and
evading his pursuers among the houses and

enclosures he reached the outer fence, over which he climbed in safety and turned to rush down the hill. But the only path bristled with spears: his enemies were pressing upon him: one chance for life remained. The pa stood on the edge of a cliff: by leaping down upon the beach below he might escape: he made the attempt; and a shout of triumph rose from his foes when they saw his body extended upon the sands; but their rage knew no bounds when he sprang up, and in a loud voice defied them to track the swift feet of the son of Tahu. To allay the suspicions of those whom he met as he fled along the coast, he gave out that he was returning for something forgotten at the last camping-place, and thus successfully passed on to Waipapa. The Ngatimamoe now proceeded to kill and eat the victims of their treachery.

The Ngai Tahu were quite unmanned by the startling intelligence brought by Tahua. After Manawa's friendly reception on a previous visit to Pakihi, they were unprepared for this act of revenge for the death of Tukiauau's father. They determined to let a year pass before they avenged the death of their chief, fearing lest a panic might seize them should they fight at once on ground where blood dear to them had been so recently spilt. They preferred waiting till the grass had overgrown the oven in which Manawa was cooked, and hidden all traces of his sad fate. When that time arrived a war party was summoned, and it was decided to proceed by sea. All the chiefs except Te Kaue were ready on the appointed day, and he was told to follow. Vexed at being left behind he urged his men to hasten the fittings of his canoe, and as soon as they were completed he launched forth and sailed in quest of his friends. On the second day he saw their fires, but passing by them landed on a point which served to conceal his canoe, but from which he could watch the Ngatimamoe pa. Seeing the enemy leaving the shore to fish in the morning he waited till they anchored, and then, issuing from his retreat, charged down upon them. He succeeded in capturing one canoe, and having killed all on board except the chief, he paddled back to the place where he had last seen his comrade's fires. They took him at first for an enemy and were not a little surprised when they recognised the very man whom they were waiting for. Seeing he had a prisoner with him, they asked who he was. "Tukaroua," replied Kaue. "He is my brother-in-law," shouted Maru, who came running down to the edge of the water with a mat* to cover him. Kaue, fearing the captive's life would be spared, stooped down and bit off his right ear and ate it. "Oh! oh!" cried the man. "Aha," said Kaue. "Did Manawa cry out when he was struck?" and stooping down, he bit the other ear off. The brother-in-law seeing Kaue's determination to

---

* If a chief wished to spare a particular prisoner he threw one of his garments over him.

retaliate Manawa's death upon the prisoner, reluctantly gave him up to be eaten. The next day Ngai Tahu laid siege to Pakihi, but its strong position baffled every effort made to take it. Food failed besiegers and besieged. The Ngai Tahu were about to retire, when Tu te rangi apiapi *who was related to persons in the pa*, hit upon a plan for its destruction. Without divulging his design he asked permission to visit the Ngatimamoe for the ostensible purpose of offering conditions of peace. He was well received by the besieged and his visits became frequent and long continued. The Ngai Tahu grew impatient at the delay and wanted to know how he was going to effect his object. "Wait," he said, "till a nor'wester blows, and then seize the opportunity afforded to you." When the wind blew from the desired quarter Tu te rangi apiapi went as usual and seated himself in the doorway of a "kauta," near the lower end of the pa and on the windward side. Having procured one of the long stones with which the women prepared fern-root for food, he fastened one end to a piece of green flax and put the other into a fire; when it was red hot he watched his opportunity and slung it into the thatch of an adjoining house. A cry of fire soon arose. The unsuspected perpetrator of the deed rushed out to assist the crowds who were trying to extinguish the flames, but in his apparent haste to pull off the burning thatch, he threw it in such a manner that the wind might blow it on to the other houses, and in a few moments the whole place was involved in the conflagration. Under cover of the smoke, the Ngai Tahu entered and a general massacre ensued. Amongst those who fled was Tu mataiao. Tu te uretira, mindful of this warrior's boast on a former occasion when he succeeded in escaping from him, pursued after him, and this time caught him. "Let me live," he begged. "Ah! was it not you who said I could not catch by morning the feet moving like the swift quivering raupo? Come with me to the camp." Arrived there, Maru beckoned for Tu mataiao to be brought to his side, where he made room for him on his mat. The poor wretch thought his life was now safe, when to his dismay "Maru the merciful" rose up, and, addressing the tribe, said—" Here take your food. Tu mataiao was then seized and put to death.

Weakened by successive defeats, the Ngatimamoe gradually retired southwards; and we do not hear of their making any very determined stand between the fall of Pakihi, or Pari whakatau, and the battle on the banks of the Aparima thirty years afterwards, when their forces were completely annihilated; although constant petty encounters between the two contending tribes continued up to the very last. It was during this interval that the fugitives from Pakihi are said to have lived in caves. Traces of their occupation are found in the rude drawings which cover the "rock shelters" at the Weka Pass, Opihi Gorge and the Upper Waitaki. The reason given for their choosing such places of abode was that they thought they were less likely to be attacked there, and if they were they would be in a better position to escape. Tukiauau, who escaped from Pakihi with his son and a few followers, separated from the main body of fugitives and went down to the Waihora lake in Otago, where he built a pa. While there his son Koroki whiti made the acquaintance of Haki te kura, the daughter of the chief whose pa stood at the mouth of the Taiari. This maiden, unknown to her friends, used to meet her lover "on the sands when the tide was low," and these clandestine meetings continued up to the time of Tukiauau's departure further south; for that chief disturbed by the rumours that reached him respecting the movements of Ngai Tahu determined to place himself beyond pursuit. Accordingly he abandoned his pa at Waihora, and embarked with his followers in a large war canoe. As they were passing below her father's pa, Haki te kura eager to join her lover, jumped off the cliff into the water; but in doing so, either fell upon a rock or on the edge of the canoe and was killed. Tu wiri roa, overwhelmed with grief and rage at the loss of his daughter swore to destroy the man who was the cause of her death. Waiting for a little while to lull suspicion, he followed in Tukiauau's wake, but could not for a long time discover his retreat, which was at length betrayed by the smoke of a fire on the island of Rakiura (Stewarts). Concealing himself behind some islets, he waited till a canoe, manned by a large number of persons, came out to fish; when they had anchored, and their attention was fixed upon their lines, Tu wiri roa bore down upon them and cut off their escape. Taken unawares without their weapons, the crew were easily overpowered and put to death, and all their companions on shore soon afterwards shared their fate.

It does not appear that the chief WAI-TAI, after separating himself from the main body of Ngai Tahu and fixing his residence in the south, was ever as successful in his encounters with Ngatimamoe as those whom he deserted were; for whilst they made a clean sweep of their opponents, driving them steadily down the coast before them, Waitai seems to have been content to plant stations here and there amongst Ngatimamoe without attempting their subjugation. We find him in alliance with Te Rangi tau neke, and joining with him in expeditions against Te Rapuwai or Waitaha who were still numerous inland. Thirty years after the conquest of the northern part of the island, the Ngatimamoe tribe was still so strong in the south that they threatened the existence of the Ngai Tahu settlements there.

Amongst the most noted chiefs who followed in WAITAI's wake was Te Wera, who for a

time occupied a strong position at the mouth of
the Waikouaiti river. He is more distinguished
for his achievements against his own tribe in
the south than against the common enemy.
He finally settled at Rakiura, where he lived
principally on seal's flesh and grew very fat.
At the "Neck," a place called the "Fright of
Te Wera" is pointed out where his first
encounter with a seal took place; when he
confessed that he, who never knew what fear
was when fighting with men, felt afraid when
fighting a "fish." On his death-bed he advised
his family to return to the mainland, "that they
might lie on a fragrant bed, and not on a fetid
one like his." An oven being in his estimation
a more desirable resting place for the body of
man than a grave.

Chapter V.

WE now enter on the second period of the Ngai Tahu occupation, the first having closed with the fall of Pakihi and the dispersion of its inhabitants. The invaders now held entire possession of the country from Wairau southwards as far as Waihora, and occupied fortified pas here and there throughout the Ngatimamoe country as far south as Rakiura.

The second period opens with the arrival, about the year 1727, of a party of young chiefs at Kaiapoi, known as the Wharaunga puraho nui, or colonising noblemen, consisting of the sons of the principal Ngai Tahu chiefs, some of whom had been brought up in the other island by their KAHU-NUNU relations. Amongst them were the sons of Turakautahi. This chief had selected Kaiapoi as his residence, where he established a reputation for hospitality—a virtue which on his death-bed he enjoined his posterity to continue the practice of for ever.

These young chiefs having ascertained from persons familiar with the physical features of the country the names of the various localities, proceeded to divide the unallotted parts of the country amongst themselves; and their procedure on this occasion is of particular interest, as it serves to illustrate one method by which the Maoris acquired title to land.

Kakapo skins were at that time highly prized, and everyone of the party was desirous to secure a parrot preserve for himself. As they approached the mountain known as Whata arama, they each claimed a peak of the range. "That is mine," cried Moki, "that my daughter Te ao tukia may possess a kilt of kakapo skins to make her fragrant and beautiful." "Mine," cried Tane tiki, "that the kakapo skins may form a kilt for my daughter Hine mihi." "Mine," cried Hikatutae, "that the kakapo skins may form a girdle for my daughter Kaiata." Moki, one of the party had his servant with him, who whispered in his ear, "Wait, do not claim anything yet;" and then the man climbed up into a tree. "What are you doing?" said the rest of the party. "Only breaking off the dry branches to light our fire with;" but he was in reality looking out for the mountain which Turakautahi had told his master was the place where the kakapo were most abundant. Presently he espied the far-famed peak. "My mountain Kura tawhiti!" he cried. "Ours!" said Moki. The claim was at once recognised by the other members of the exploring expedition, and Moki's descendants have ever since enjoyed the exclusive right to catch kakapo on Kura tawhiti.

Hostilities against Ngatimamoe were renewed on the arrival of these young chiefs and the infusion of new blood into the Ngai Tahu war counsels. An expedition under the command of Moki was sent in the canoe Makawhiua against Parakakariki on the south-eastern side of the peninsula. After destroying that pa, Moki returned to Koukourarata, where he landed and proceeded over the hills to Waikakahi, where Tu te kawa, who killed his grandfather's wives, was still living, though now a very old man. This chief, whose flight south has already been mentioned, settled first at Okohana because eels were plentiful there; but finding those of Waihora were of a better quality, he removed to the shores of that lake, and built a pa at Waikakahi, while his son Te Rangitamau built another at Taumutu. Surrounded by his allies, and at such a great distance from his enemies, Tu te kawa thought himself quite safe; but the avenger of blood was already on his track, and he was doomed to die a violent death. But the end came when least expected by himself and his people, for the first intimation they had of any immediate danger was when they saw Moki and his men inside their pa. The old chief, infirm and helpless, was found coiled up in his mats in a corner of his house, and a natural impulse prompted Moki and his brothers at the last moment to shield their kinsman, but the avenger of blood thrust his spear between them, and plunged it into the old man's body.

Having ascertained that his son was away at Taumutu, and not knowing what course he might take, Moki gave orders that a watch should be kept during the night round the camp to guard against surprise, but his orders were disregarded. Te Rangitamau, whose suspicions were aroused by observing a more than ordinary quantity of smoke arising from the neighbourhood of his father's pa, set off at once for the place, which he reached after dark. Passing through the sleeping warriors, he approached his father's house, and looking in saw his own wife Puna hikoia sitting by the fire. Stepping inside, he touched her gently on the shoulder, and putting his finger to his lips as a signal to keep silence, beckoned her to come outside. There he questioned her about what had happened; and finding that she and his children had been kindly treated, he told his wife to wake Moki after he was gone, and to give him this message, "Your life was in my hands, but I gave it back to you." Then taking off his dog-skin mat he placed it across Moki's knees, and hurried away to his own stronghold on the hill close by. When Puna hikoia thought her husband safe from pursuit, she woke Moki and gave him the message. Moki felt the mat, and was convinced the woman spoke the truth. He was greatly mortified at being caught sleeping, as it was always injurious to a warrior's reputation to be discovered off his guard. Issuing from the whare he roused his sleeping followers with the words which have since become proverbial, " Ngai tuwhaitara mata hori." " Ngai tuwhaitara with eyes that deceive :" in allusion to their having permitted an enemy to pass unchallenged through their lines. The next day negotiations were entered into with Te Rangitamau and peace restored between him and his kinsmen.

It is not till the Ngai Tahu conquests reached Horowhenua that we hear anything of Ngati Wairangi, the tribe occupying the west coast, who, like Ngatimamoe and Ngai Tahu, were descendants of Tura, and crossed over to this island almost at the same time with them. Hitherto they had been shut off from communication with the east coast by what were thought to be impassable natural barriers, till a mad woman, named Raureka, discovered a way through them. Wandering from her home, this woman went up the bed of the Hokitika river, and then across what is known as Browning's Pass, and thence down to the east coast. There in the neighbourhood of Horowhenua she came upon some men engaged in shaping a canoe, and taking notice of their tools remarked how very blunt they were. The men asked if she knew of any better. She replied by taking a little packet from her bosom, which she carefully unfolded, and displayed a sharp fragment of greenstone. This was the first specimen of that stone which the natives there had ever seen, and they were so delighted with the discovery that they sent a party immediately over the ranges to fetch some ; and it subsequently came into general use for edged tools and weapons, those made of inferior materials being discarded. If Raureka was a co-temporary of Moki she arrived at Horowhenua about the year 1700.

It does not follow from this account of the introduction of greenstone that it was quite unknown at that period to the Maoris living in other parts of the country : for the Hawaikians knew of its existence in this island long before they came to live here, having heard about it from the celebrated navigator Ngahue, who was the first to discover New Zealand. He made the discovery when trying to escape from a powerful and vindictive woman named Hine tuao hoanga, whose ill will he had incurred. He escaped from her on the back of his Sea God named Poutini. He first sighted Tuhua (Mayor Island), and then Ao-te-aroa, but fearing that those places were too close to his enemy who was he knew in pursuit of him ; he continued his voyage till he reached the mouth of the River Arahura, where he settled and found the greenstone. Ngahue was so convinced of its value that he ventured to return to Hawaiki with a cargo of the stone ; trusting that the service which he was rendering his countrymen, by bringing such a useful material to their knowledge, would ensure their favour and protection. It is said that it was with axes made of this greenstone that the canoes were shaped which brought the first Maori immigrants to this country. Although much of this story must be rejected as fabulous it is quite possible that Ngahue's Sea God may have been a proa or junk, as European vessels when first seen, were called "atuas" by the Maoris. The descendants of Maru tuahu at Hauraki show a hei tiki, which they say he wore when he arrived in New Zealand. It has been handed down from generation to generation, being alternately in possession of his Taranaki and Hauraki descendants. It is quite possible, too, that traffic in greenstone between Ngati Wairangi and the North Island tribes bordering on Cook Straits may have been in existence for many years before it became known to Ngai Tahu.

The discovery of greenstone brought Ngati Wairangi into collision with Ngai Tahu, and blood was shed. To avenge this, Turakautahi asked Te Rangitamau to undertake the command of an expedition, which he accepted. The route chosen was up the Rakaia, with which locality Te Rangitamau was familiar. Somewhere between Kanieri and Kokatahi he fell in with Te Uekanuka, a chief celebrated as much for his enormous size as for his great courage, whom he killed. Having accomplished his object Te Rangitamau returned. The next expedition was attended with very disastrous results, being defeated by Ngati Wairangi at Mahinapua, where Tane tiki, Tu te pirirangi,

GREENSTONE ORNAMENT.

and Tutae maro were slain ; the survivors with difficulty effecting their retreat.

To avenge this loss a third expedition was sent under the command of Moki and Maka, who defeated Ngati Wairangi at Otuku whakaoka. The struggle between the two tribes continued till within the last fifty years, when Tuhuru and his brother Te Pare overcame Ngati Wairangi at the battle of Paparoa, and, assisted by Te ao whakamaru and Puku, completed their destruction. The present residents on the coast are Ngai Tahu.

The sons of Turakautahi, who were eager to emulate the brave deeds of the Hataitai warriors, determined to follow up their successes and complete the conquest of the Ngatimamoe. They planned a raid on the south, and Kaweriri was placed in chief command. On crossing the Waitaki the force divided into two parts, one proceeded by an inland road, the other along the coast ; by this manœuvre they succeeded in driving those of the Ngatimamoe who were not in alliance with Ngai Tahu hapus before them, till they reached Aparima, where, at Tara hau kapiti, or Wai tara mea, they were brought to bay. Both sides displayed the greatest courage, and for a while the issue of the struggle was uncertain. To the consternation of Ngai Tahu, their leader and foremost warrior, Kaweriri, was mortally wounded by Tu te makohu, and for a moment they wavered, but observing that they rallied again, that chief dreading the consequences of his deed retired from the field; but he was observed and pursued by a young warrior, Te mai werohia, who thought to earn a reputation by avenging the death of his leader. Hearing the sound of footsteps Tu te makohu turned and asked who it was that was following him. On hearing the name and recognising it, he asked whether his pursuer was the son of Kiri teka teka (a relative of his own married to a Ngai Tahu). When told that he was, he said " Turn back, lest you fall by the hand of your mother's kinsman." In the meantime Parakiore having recovered from the shock produced by his brother's death, was now in hot pursuit of Tu te makohu, and this parley afforded the opportunity of overtaking him. The fugitive was making his way up a steep hill-side, and already heard the hard quick breathing of his pursuer when he invoked the aid of his atua, who caused a friendly mist to descend and hide him from pursuit : reminding us of the scene on the plains of Troy, when Menelaus with

"vindictive strides rushed again."
"On Paris spear in hand, but him involved
In mist opaque, Venus with ease divine
Snatched thence."

Ngatimamoe being defeated retired some miles up the river, where they took up a fortified position, and being still superior to their assailants in number hoped to make a successful stand. But their hopes were doomed to disappointment, for in a few days they were again attacked, and after a desperate resistance defeated with great slaughter at Teihoka, where, till quite recently, the bleaching bones witnessed to the numbers of the slain. The few who escaped fled into the forests towards the west, across the lake Te Anau.

Those portions of the tribe scattered along the coast from Otakou to the southern sounds, were in the course of a few years destroyed or absorbed by the Ngai Tahu ; and the Ngatimamoe, as a distinct and independent tribe, may be said to have perished at Teihoka. Those who were in alliance with Ngai Tahu were still numerous, but their position was felt to be so insecure that, on the return of Turakautahi's sons from their successful raid, Te Rangi ihia, a noted Ngatimamoe chief residing at Matau, determined to proceed to Kaiapoi, and make lasting terms of peace with the conquerors. He was kindly received ; and, to cement the treaty then made, Hine hakiri, one of the ruling family of Ngai Tahu, was given to him in marriage ; and his own sister, Kohiwai, was married to Hone kai, son of Te Hau. Rangi ihia resided with his wife's relations till after the birth of his son Pari, when they advised him to return, as it was their wish to embody Rangi ihia's hapu with their own, and to make the boy chief of both. Te Hau and Turakautahi's sons escorted Rangi ihia to the south.

On reaching home he was shocked to see one of his sisters cooking food like a common slave.

When leaving her behind, he had taken care to provide such attendance as befitted her rank, and he could not account for her being reduced to such straits as to be obliged to cook her own food. Suppressing his indignation till night-fall, he took the opportunity when all was quiet of asking her why she had so demeaned herself. She then told him that, after he left, her maids married and deserted her. Seizing his weapons, Rangi ihia, having ascertained where they were to be found, went to the house occupied by the runaways and killed both the women. As he turned his back to go out again, one of the husbands drove a spear into his shoulder, the point breaking off against the bone. On reaching his own whare, Te Hau pulled this out with his teeth, and applied a toetoe plaster to the wound. While Rangi ihia was recovering, he unfortunately sneered at the weakness of the arm which had struck him : " Had it been my own the thrust would have been fatal." This coming to the ears of the injured men, they scraped the end of the spear and got off the dry blood adhering to it, and, by performing incantations over it, produced symptoms of madness in Rangi ihia, who shortly afterwards died. Before his death, he turned to his friend Te Hau and said, " When I am gone do not let my brothers live ; they are bitter men, and will slay my children." It was at Otepoti where he was being treated for his wound and died. His brothers and their people were camped at a short distance off at the other end of the bay. On calling out one morning to ask how the patient was, their suspicions were roused by the way in which the answer was given. The person replying cried out, "He is——," and then paused suddenly as if being remonstrated with, finishing the sentence by saying—"gone with his wife and children." Having no reasons to distrust the professions of friendship made by their chief's connections a party of Ngatimamoe entered the Ngai Tahu camp shortly afterwards when Te Hau, mindful of the dying chief's charge, fell upon his two brothers, Taihua and Te Rangiamohia, and killed them. Te Rangi ihia was buried in accordance with his own desire on the summit of Te raka a runga te raki, " that his spirit might see from thence his old haunts to the southward."

His wife and children were sent back to their friends in the north, while Te Hau took up his quarters at Pukekura, where he was subsequently attacked by a large force of Ngatimamoe. During the siege of his pa one of the most renowned of his warriors, a man named TARE-WAI, was caught outside, while reconnoitring the enemy's position. He was thrown upon his back by his captors and held down by a number of men while WHAKA-TAKA-NEWHA, the commander of the Ngatimamoe, proceeded to cut him open with a sharp stone knife. The operation began by scoring the skin from the throat down to the pit of the stomach, but

Tarewai never winced, as he did not wish to make the men who were holding him tighten their grasp, but as the knife was passing down the groove the second time, and had just penetrated the cavity below his ribs, he gave a loud shout and sprang so suddenly to his feet that, before his enemies could realise what had happened, he was lost in the cover of the neighbouring woods, and, though hotly pursued, was never overtaken. Having found a suitable hiding place, Tarewai proceeded to doctor his wounds, to which he applied plasters of leaves, supporting life during the process as best he could on fern root and small birds. As soon as his wounds were sufficiently healed he made his way back to the neighbourhood of the Ngatimamoe camp, which he entered without being detected under the cover of darkness. He happened to approach a group of chiefs who were examining by the firelight the very weapon which they had taken from him. He heard them mention his own name, and, as they passed the weapon of whalebone-ivory from hand to hand, they praised the beauty of it. Edging close up to the speakers, he said " Let me too look at the weapon of this brave warrior." As soon as it was handed to him he darted off into the bush where he was soon lost sight of in the darkness.

The next day Tarewai managed to get close enough to the pa to be recognised by the inmates, who were rejoiced to find that he was still alive. Climbing up a tree at the rear of the Ngatimamoe Camp, he clapped his hands and flourished his white weapon in such a way as to indicate to his friends that he wanted them to engage in a war dance. When they had ranged themselves for it, he waved his hand toward the seaward side of the pa, showing that that was where he wanted the dance to take place. When it began the Ngatimamoe flocked to that end of their camp to watch it. This gave Tarewai a chance of reaching the sandy beach below Taiaroa Head unobserved, and he was not slow to avail himself of it, but just when he thought himself safe from pursuit, he almost jumped into the arms of two old men who were mending a canoe on the beach, who pursued him so hotly that when he reached the rocks if it had not been for an overhanging bush which he caught hold of, and by which he swung himself clear of his pursuers on to the cliff above, he would have been taken prisoner a second time. His marvellous escape so inspirited his friends that they resolved to make an immediate attack upon their besiegers, whom they defeated and drove away.

Many years after Rangi ihia's death, his bones were carried down by a landslip to the beach, where they were picked up by a Ngai Tahu man who made a fish-hook of one of them and when using it made some insolent remark about the old man on the hill holding the hapuku well. A Ngatimamoe who was present reported the words to his companions, who remarked, " The two brothers died in open fight, but this man has been dishonoured after death, and the insult must be avenged." An opportunity occurred shortly after for accomplishing their meditated act of retailation. A party had been sent from Pukekura to Rauone to collect fern-root. One of them Tane toro tika, the son of Taoka and grandson of Manawa, a young chief of very high rank, was surprised and taken prisoner; on being carried to the presence of Te Maui, that chief seeing him said, " This comb-fastening is equal to that comb-fastening," meaning that the captive's rank corresponded to that of the chief whose remains had been desecrated, and thereupon killed him. Tai kawa, a Ngai Tahu warrior, immediately after the deed, came upon the band of Ngatimamoe and asked them what had become of their prisoner. When told that they had killed him, he said, " You have done foolishly, for not a soul of you will now be spared; you will be banished to the haunts of the Moho Notornis Mantelli and in the depths of the forest will be your only place of safety."

This threat was soon after carried into effect by Te Hau, who, after a series of engagements, drove the remnants of Ngatimamoe into the dense forests that cover the south-western coast, where further pursuit was useless. Traces of these fugitives have been met with up to a very recent date.

About seventy years ago Te Rimu rapa, while on his way to plunder a sealing-station, discovered a woman who called herself Tu ai te kura ; finding that she was a Ngatimamoe, he cruelly killed and devoured her there and then. About six years afterwards, Te wae wae surprised two men while he was out eel-spearing near Aparima, but they escaped before he could catch them. In 1842 a sealing party, while pulling up one of the sounds, observed smoke issuing from the face of a cliff. Climbing to the spot they found a cave evidently just deserted. It was partitioned across the middle—the inner part being used as a sleeping place, the outer for cooking. They found a handsome feather-mat, and a patu paraoa, some fish-hooks, and some flax-baskets in process of making. An attempt was made to pursue the late inmates of the cave, but it had to be abandoned, because the undergrowth in the forest was so dense, and the paths so numerous, that the pursuers were afraid of being lost in the maze or falling into an ambuscade ; they, therefore, returned to the boat, carrying with them the articles which they found in the cave. These were exhibited at Otakou, Banks Peninsula, and Kaiapoi. The mat was sent to Otaki, and the patu paraoa was eventually given to me by Muru, an old chief of Port Levy.

Aperahama Hutoitoi of Nga whakaputaputa affirms that twenty-four years ago, when sealing in the sounds, he saw smoke in the distance, and visiting the spot the next day observed the footprints of several persons on the sands, evidently Maoris from the shape of the feet.

Having suffered so cruelly from Ngai Tahu, the survivors of the persecuted tribe seem to be always in a state of flight, imagining that their ancient foes are still in pursuit. Though the country has of late years been well explored by " prospecting" parties without any people being found, it is just possible that a small remnant may still remain secreted in the recesses of that inaccessible region.

The Ngaitahu having triumphed over all their enemies and obtained possession of the whole of the South Island (with the exception of a small strip bordering on Cook's Strait), their historical traditions from this period till the capture of Kaiapohia by RAUPARAHA in 1828, contain nothing of special interest to the general reader, and may very well be omitted from this short sketch of their history.

Chapter VI.

THE historical traditions contain so little information about the ordinary habits of life and thought amongst the Maori people, that unless that want is supplied from traditions of another class, the reader is in danger of forming a very erroneous opinion of Maori acquirements and character. I purpose, therefore, to refer in this concluding chapter to some of those traditions which seem best calculated to illustrate the national characteristics of thought and action.

I shall commence with a brief review of the mythological traditions, which, according to no less an authority than Professor Max Müller, "contain much that will deeply interest all those who have learned to sympathise with the childhood of the world, and have not forgotten that the child is the father of the man; much that will startle those who think that metaphysical conceptions are incompatible with downright savagery; much also that will comfort those who hold that God has not left Himself without a witness even amongst the lowest outcasts of the human race." It is, indeed, surprising to find a people, sunk in such barbarism as the Maoris were at the time when they first came into contact with Europeans, possessing such elaborate theories about the origin of all things —theories which contain traces of a philosophy which evidently belonged to a period of higher mental culture. They conceived of the lapse of countless ages before the dawn of light upon the earth. Commencing with Te Kore, or Nothingness, to which they assign an unlimited period, they approach the dawn of Life and Consciousness on earth through eighteen stages, each stage being a period of myriads of years. "Then began the first Seeking and Searching." Hence the saying of antiquity,—

> Darkness, Darkness ;
> Light, Light ;
> The Seeking, the Searching,
> In Chaos, in Chaos.

This was the seeking for a consciousness of existence and freedom of action.

In the order of existence, the Maoris believed that Thought came first, then Spirit, and last of all Matter.

Living beings existed from an inconceivably distant past, when everything was wrapped in darkness. Heaven, or Sky, was the father, and Earth the mother of all. In order to deepen the impression in men's minds of the vast length of the period preceding the dawn of creation, instead of stating the fact in so many words, the traditions enumerate the several periods, counting from the first to the tenth, and from the tenth to the hundredth, and from the hundredth to the thousandth, and from the thousandth to myriads. And this was repeated eighteen times while describing the slow progress from a past eternity to the dawn of light, and the creation of animal and vegetable life.

How light reached the Earth is thus told: After countless ages, during which Heaven and Earth adhered to one another, their offspring, weary of the darkness in which they were enveloped, conspired to rend them asunder. Five of the boldest undertook, each in turn, the task; Tane alone was successful. Planting his head firmly on his mother's body, he raised his feet upwards and pressed them against his father, and by a mighty effort he rent his parents apart, in spite of their shrieks and cries. The legend concludes with a very beautiful conception of the origin of mists and dewdrops.

"The vast Heaven has still ever remained separated from his spouse the Earth. Yet their mutual love still continues—the soft warm sighs of her loving bosom still ever rise up to him, ascending from the wooded mountains and valleys, and men call these mists; and the vast Heaven, as he mourns through the long nights his separation from his beloved, drops frequent tears upon her bosom, and men, seeing these, term them dewdrops." (Sir G. Grey, Poly. Myth., p. 15.)

It is a noticeable fact that, with the exception of Mother Earth, no female deities are spoken of amongst the chief gods in connection with the beginning of things, though they appear later on in the history of the world. During the period between the separation of earth and sky and the appearance of man, this world was occupied by the race of demi-gods, whose existence was discovered at the time of the separation. It is to this period that the exploits of such heroes as Maui and Tawhaki relate. It is from what is told about them we learn that the Maoris conceived of an under and upper world, earth lying between them. When Maui sought to discover who his father was he resolved to follow his mother Taranga, who nightly visited her children on earth, but vanished again before dawn. To discover the path by which she went, Maui determined to detain her till it was light enough to watch her movements; so he carefully closed every crevice through which light could enter the building where his mother slept, and, on her waking and wondering at the prolonged darkness, he quieted her by the assurance that it was still night. But when the sun rose high in the heavens a sunbeam shot in through a chink, and Taranga with a shriek sprang out of the house. Maui watched her seize a tuft of grass, and descend an opening beneath it. By magic he changed himself into a pigeon, and followed his mother. After a long flight down a narrow cavern, he emerged

into open space, and saw before him a party of
people seated under a grove of trees, and
amongst them his mother, and beside her a
man who he at once surmised was his father.
Eventually he was recognised, and the mother
told how she had prematurely given birth to
him by the sea-shore, when she cut off her long
tresses, and, having bound him in them, cast
him into the foam of the sea, where he was
found by a sea-god, and reared up by him.
The father thereupon acknowledged him, and
proceeded to baptise him ; but, owing to the
omission of some part of the rite, Maui became
subject to the "Great Lady of Night" (Death).

Besides believing in an inhabited Under
world the Maoris believed in an inhabited
Upper world, consisting of ten planes, one
above the other. In the highest resided Rehua,
the Aged One, with flowing locks, and lightning
flashing from his armpits. He was the eldest
son of Rangi, and supreme lord of the gods
who ruled the world. He was the Lord of
Kindness, and dispersed gloom and sadness.
He was opposed to war and bloodshed. "The
darting lightning," says an ancient poem,
"gleams above and Rehua commands where
all that sacred is." (White, vol i., p. 37.) The
descriptions of Rehua continually recall to mind
the Olympian Jove, "Father of gods and men."

That the Maoris conceived of the gods as
something more than the embodiments of power
—as beings taking an interest in human affairs,

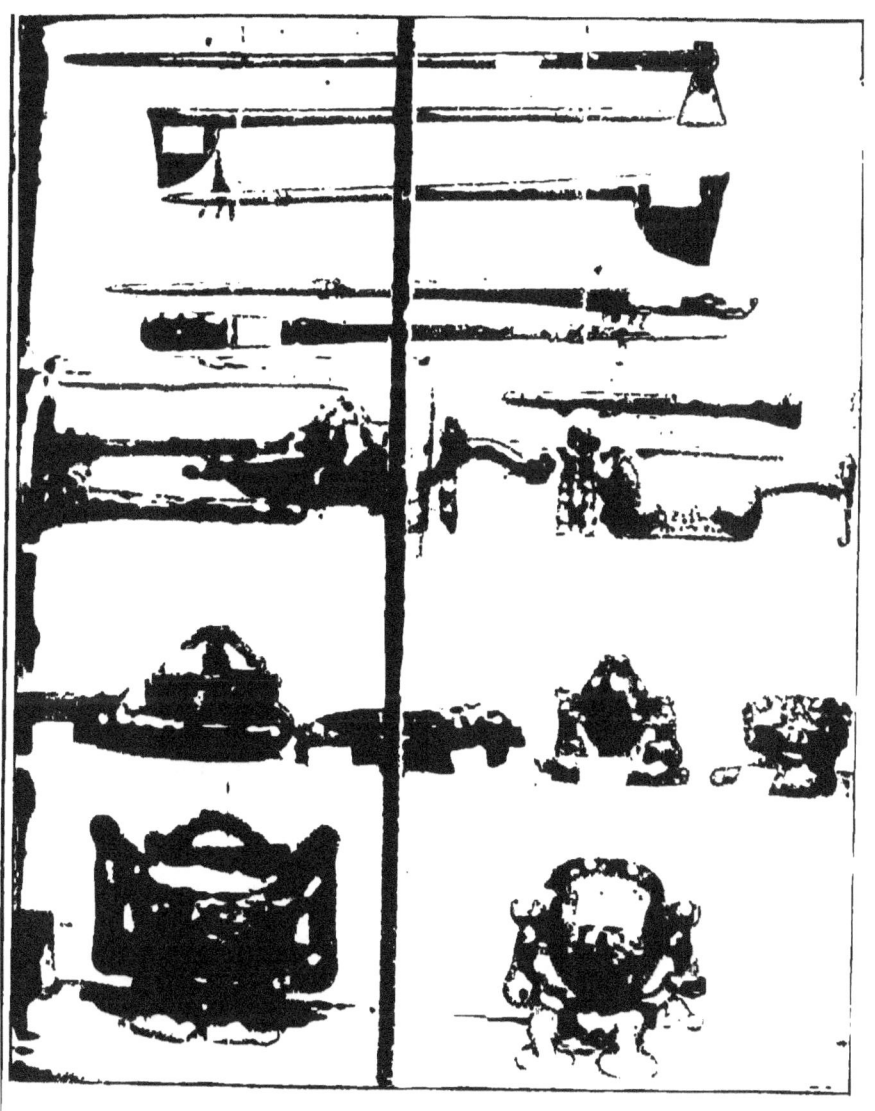

SPECIMENS OF CARVED BOXES, WEAPONS, ETC.

and able to see and hear from the highest of the heavens what took place on earth—is indicated by the story of Maui's elder brother going in search of his elder sister Hinauri. In the course of his search he ascended the heavens to consult Rehua and get the clue to her whereabouts. On reaching the first heaven he asked the dwellers there, "Are the heavens above this inhabited?" They answered, "They are." He again forced his way upwards, and found an inhabited place, and he asked those he met whether the heavens above them were inhabited. They said, "Yes." He continued his ascent, asking the same question and receiving the same answer, till he reached the Tenth Heaven, the abode of the God Rehua. "Rupe feared the Man of Ancient Days, and at length ventured to say, 'O Rehua! has a confused murmur of voices from the world below reached you upon any subject regarding which I am interested?' The god answered, 'Yes, such a murmuring of distant voices has reached me from the Sacred Isle Motutapu in the world below.'" When Rupe heard this he immediately changed himself into a pigeon, and took flight downwards towards the island of Motutapu, where he found his beloved sister.

Sometimes the inhabitants of the upper world, who were superior in beauty and acquirements to those who dwelt on earth, fell in love with men; and some very charming stories are told of these attachments, reminding the reader of the Eastern legends of the loves of the angels, so beautifully told by the poet Thomas Moore. The fame of the hero Tawhaki's courage and manly beauty chanced to reach the ears of a young maiden of the heavenly race who lived above in the skies. One night she descended to judge for herself. She found him lying asleep. After gazing at him she stole to his side, but before dawn she went back to the heavens. She repeated her visits night after night till love forced her to disclose herself fully, and for her lover's sake she forsook her friends and her home in the sky. After a time a daughter was born to them. Tawhaki, shortly after its birth, made some disparaging remark about the child, which pained the mother so deeply that she seized the babe, and took flight upwards. Tawhaki tried to seize her, and prevent her going, crying out, " Mother of my child, oh ! return once more to me." But as she soared upwards she replied, " No, no, I shall never return to you again." "At least, then, leave me some parting token of remembrance," he cried. " My parting words," she said, " are lay fast hold on that creeper which, hanging down from on high, has again struck its fibres into the earth." Tawhaki was plunged in grief, his heart torn by regrets for his wife and little girl. Unable to endure their loss, he went in search of them, accompanied by his younger brother. They journeyed on till they reached the spot where the ends of the tendrils, which hung down from heaven, reached the earth, and there they found an old ancestress, quite blind, named the Face of Night. She was the keeper of the tendrils which hung from above, and sat at the spot where they touched the earth, and held the end of one of them in her hands. The two brothers adopted a curious device to obtain from the old lady the information they wanted ; and, having succeeded, the younger brother was the first to attempt the ascent. He sprang into the air, but seized by mistake a loose tendril, and away he swung to the very edge of the horizon ; but a blast of wind drove him in an opposite direction, and so he swung backwards and forwards till, his feet touching the earth again, he let go his hold and gave up the attempt. Tawhaki then seized a firmly-rooted tendril, and began to climb. By direction of his old relative, the Face of Night, he kept on repeating powerful incantations, and so escaped the dangers of that difficult and terrible road, and reached the sky. Then the legend describes how he transformed himself into an ugly old man, and joined a party of people who were making canoes, who pressed him into their service, and made him carry their tools and firewood, and how he horrified them all when they reached the village by seating himself beside the sacred person of the chief lady of the place, who was no other than his celestial wife. After exciting the wonder and curiosity of all the inhabitants of the place, he made himself known to his wife, and resumed his natural appearance. He never returned to earth again, and was worshipped by the Maoris as the God of Thunder and Lightning.

How mankind learnt to ignite fire is told in a curious legend common to all Polynesians. The Maori Prometheus, Maui, who was a great practical joker, having extinguished all existing fires, his mother directed the servants to go and ask the goddess Mahuika to give them fire to cook with, but they were all too terrified to obey her. Maui then offered to go himself. His parents warned him not to play any tricks on the old lady, and he promised to be careful. But on reaching the abode of the Goddess of Fire, and obtaining what he asked for, he went aside and extinguished it, and presented himself again. The fire was obtained by the goddess from the root of her nails, which she tore out to obtain it. Maui kept on extinguishing the fire given, and asking for more, till he thoroughly exasperated the Fire Goddess, who, when reduced to her last toe-nail, pulled it out and dashed it to the ground, when everything caught fire. Maui changed himself into a hawk, and flew with rapid flight ; but the earth and sea caught fire, and Maui narrowly escaped destruction. The fire was extinguished by the aid of the God of storms. But before the fire was all lost the Fire Goddess saved some sparks, which she threw into the kaikomako and a few other trees, where they are still cherished. Hence men rub portions of the wood of these trees together when they wish to ignite a fire.

The inhabitants of earth became subject to death through Maui's failure to overcome the Great Lady of Night. Maui, having overcome every labour he undertook, asked his father whether there was any undertaking beyond his power. He replied, "It is impossible for you to overcome your ancestress, the Great Lady of Night." Maui replied, "Lay aside such idle thoughts, and let us both fearlessly seek whether men are to die or live for ever." Boasting of the great feats he had accomplished, Maui went forth, full of confidence, to attempt the conquest of the devourer of all living. Accompanied by a crowd of companions, disguised as little birds, he reached the dwelling of the old lady in the evening. She was asleep, with her mouth wide open. Divesting himself of his clothing, and armed with a weapon, he entered the old woman's mouth. The little birds tried hard to suppress their laughter at the ridiculous figure he cut. At last the tiwakawaka (fantail) could keep his merriment in no longer, and laughed out loudly. This woke the old woman, who, discovering her danger, closed her mouth on Maui, who never returned to this world again. And in consequence of his failure death prevailed over all beings on earth.

The labours of Maui were—

1. The search for and discovery of his father in the under-world.

2. Obtaining his ancestress Muriranga-whenua's jaw-bone.
3. Noosing and beating the sun, so that mankind might have longer days.
4. Fishing up the land.
5. Fetching fire from the goddess Mahuika.
6. Changing his sister Hinauri's husband into a dog.
7. His encounter with the Great Lady of Night, in which he lost his life.

To quote Judge Fornander's remarks upon similar myths in Hawaii, "They point to a period of the human mind when the thoughts of sages still lingered and laboured on the borderland between material facts and metaphysical abstractions; when Atea was still half the sun springing forth from and succeeding to and dispelling the gloom and darkness of night, and half the deified impersonation of creative power; when Atea was still the mere dawn in the result of the apparent contest between darkness and light encircling the neck of the sun as well as his goddess-wife."

The historical traditions of the Maoris date from a period antecedent to their arrival in this country, and are full of very interesting information. Many of them relate to voyages undertaken by ancient navigators; and the description given by them of the seas through which they sailed points to the early migrations of the race in tropical latitudes.

It would occupy too much time to trace in detail the history as told in these traditions, but there are a few interesting facts contained in them which may be mentioned because they throw some light upon the origin of this remarkable people.

When asked where they came from, the Maoris of New Zealand always replied "Hawaiki." For a long time it was thought that the Hawaiki to which they referred was one of the Sandwich Islands; but when the Pacific became better known it was discovered that every group occupied by Polynesians possessed an island of that name, and that Savaii, in the Samoan group, Avaiki, in the Hervey group, Habai, of Tonga, Hawaii, of the Sandwich Islands, all bore the same name, which meant Little Hawa. Judge Fornander has taken great pains to find out the reason for the constant recurrence of this name, and I venture to think that his theory about it is correct. Tracing the course by which the Maori race reached its present home in the Pacific, he discovered that at one time it occupied the large island we call Java, a name which he thinks the Maoris brought with them from the cradle of their race in the Cushite Empire of Saba or Zaba, and gave to their island home, just as we have given Old-World names to our new homes in these southern seas. On being driven out of Java by a Malay invasion, the Maoris migrated eastward in search of new lands, and when settling in the islands they found they invariably named one Hawa, after their last home, but, to distinguish it from the original, added the adjective "iti," and called it Hawa-iti or -iki, Little Saba or Java.

It adds to our interest in the Maori people to think that they come of a race which had attained to a high state of civilisation a thousand years before our era. Their long isolation from other nations has helped them to preserve in their myths and legends, and in their religious rites and social customs, much that may assist ethnologists to solve the questions raised by the discovery of monuments and remains in the countries once occupied by Cushite civilisation, but about which the present inhabitants of those countries know nothing at all.

Emerging from the region of myths and legends, and approaching actual history, the traditions contain narratives of several voyages made by Maori explorers to New Zealand before the final migration of the present inhabitants took place.

Of these navigators the most celebrated were Ngahue, the original discoverer of New Zealand, Kupe, and Tamateapokaiwhenua. Ngahue is said to have discovered greenstone on the west coast of the South Island, and to have taken a quantity of it back with him to Hawaiki. Kupe afterwards circumnavigated the North Island, and Tamatea the South. The principal migration to these shores took place about the year A.D. 1400, or about the time when Henry V. of England gained the Battle of Agincourt.

The causes which led to the present inhabitants abandoning their former home and coming here are variously related; but the most probable tale is that, a civil war having broken out, the weaker party determined to seek refuge in the new country about which such favourable reports had been brought back to them by Ngahue, Kupe, and others. The chief body of emigrants embarked in a fleet of six or seven canoes, each capable of containing 140 men. One of these vessels, the "Arawa," is described as being formed of two canoes lashed together, a deckhouse occupying the platform which joined them. They appear to have been similar in all respects to the canoes seen by Captain Cook in the Pacific, and said to be very suitable for long voyages.

The traditions furnish internal evidence of their general correctness. For one thing, we learn from them the season of the year when the canoes reached this country. The rata was then in bloom, and one of the crew was so struck with the brilliant colour of the flowers that he threw his soiled red-feather head-dress overboard, intending to get a fresh one from the woods on landing. This tradition shows that the migration took place at the only season of the year when the prevailing winds were fair for voyagers from the north-west to the south-east.

Many other details might in like manner be cited to prove the correctness of the narrative.

Besides the first fleet, other canoes appear from time to time to have arrived from Hawaiki, bringing fresh settlers to the country. And there are accounts of return-voyages being made in search of sweet-potato seed, and the secret of its successful culture and storage.

Some idea may be formed of the mass of traditions which had accumulated in the course of centuries (and the mental effort it must have cost the people to hand down to our time even such portions as we have been able to rescue from oblivion) when we consider the voluminous nature of one class alone—namely, those relating to tribal history, and the biographical records of notable men and women

On arriving in New Zealand, or Ao-tea-roa, the crews of the colonising fleet dispersed themselves over the length and breadth of these Islands, and formed independent tribes or nations, each of which was subdivided into *hapus*, and the *hapus* into families. Each family, *hapu*, and *iwi* carefully preserved their genealogies and the record of their doings. Every free man amongst the Maoris was required to know by what title the land claimed by his tribe was held—whether by right of original occupation, conquest, purchase, or gift—and thus it happened that traditions relating to the same transactions were preserved by tribes whose interests were antagonistic.

Several opportunities have been afforded in recent times through the Native Land Court of comparing these accounts which have been transmitted for several generations through separate and independent channels, and they have almost invariably been found to agree—a fact which adds to our confidence in accepting other traditions preserved in the same way, but the accuracy of which cannot be proved in the same manner. The laws by which the Maoris regulated their social and civil relationships were embodied in the historical traditions, which served at the same time to show how these laws originated, and to illustrate their application.

Although the greater part of the annals handed down relate to intertribal wars, we must not read them by the light of our knowledge of the state of things which existed when firearms were first introduced. Those weapons revolutionised Maori warfare, and encouraged ambitious men to prosecute devastating wars, which produced a reign of terror throughout the country. During the centuries which preceded our occupation, the ordinary life of the people *in times of peace* was pleasant and agreeable. The people possessed abundance of food, and agreeable and healthy occupation for mind and body. Each season of the year and each part of the day had its allotted work or amusement both for men, women, and children. The women, besides such household duties as the preparation of food and cleansing their houses, made the clothing and bedding required for their families. They gathered the flax and ti-palm fibres used, and prepared and worked them up into a variety of garments, some of which took months to complete, and when finished were beautiful specimens of handiwork. The children played a variety of games with tops, balls, kites, and swings. The youths engaged in wrestling and running, leaping with poles, skipping in squads of ten or a dozen together, and foot- and canoe-races. The men gathered the food and stored it in *whatas* or storerooms, which were attached to every chief's compound, and built on tall posts to protect the contents from damp and rats. Besides such natural products of the soil as fern-root, ti-palm stems, convolvulus-roots, and the berries of the karaka and hinau, the Maoris cultivated the kumara, hue, and taro. Fish of various kinds were caught during the proper season, and cured in vast quantities by drying in the sun, just as the Caribs of the Mexican Gulf cured their boucan. Wild pigeons, kakas, koko, tui, Paradise ducks, wekas, and mutton-birds were cooked and preserved in their own fat, in vessels made out of large kelp-leaves. Netting, carving, and the grinding and fitting of stone implements and weapons occupied the old men, and much of the leisure time of the young. They beguiled the long winter evenings by reciting historical traditions and tribal genealogies, by repeating poetry and fairy tales, and by songs, dances, flute-playing, and round games.

"In their social and domestic relations," to quote Mr. Colenso, "much harmony and good feeling prevailed. They were courteous in their behaviour towards each other, and so unwilling to hurt the feelings of others, that in conveying bad and startling news they employed a song or quoted a saying of well-known meaning. They avoided wantonly hurting anyone's feeling, and were scrupulously careful not to cause offence to visitors by look, word, or gesture. Anyone guilty of rude behaviour was spoken of as one who had had no parents—one hatched from a cuckoo's egg. If they met an enemy in the company of one of their own friends and allies, no matter how deadly the feud between them might be, they would be quite civil to the enemy, and do nothing to harm him while with their friend, for fear of giving him pain, though, once separated from the friend's protection, they would not hesitate to kill and eat him."

Their chivalrous conduct on some occasions towards their foes was very remarkable—perhaps unparalleled except in the age of knighthood. Instances are recorded of a besieging party, when informed that their enemies were in want of food or weapons, sending a supply.

The story of Tutewaimate's encounter with the robber-chieftain Moko (found on page 25) illustrates this pleasing trait in the Maori character.

The courage and endurance of Maori warriors is abundantly illustrated; and, though the record of ferocity, cruelty, and treachery found in the traditions is often appalling, it is sometimes relieved by deeds of generosity and mercifulness. While one dying chief bequeaths to his tribe the prosecution of a blood-feud, another implores those he is leaving behind him to forgive the wrongs they have suffered, and to promote peace. Again and again we hear the echo in succeeding generations of the words uttered by a venerable father of the people as they were leaving the shores of Hawaiki: "O my children! hearken to these my words. Depart in peace, and when you reach the place you are going to, do not follow after the deeds of Tu, the god of war, but rather follow quiet and useful occupations, and then you will die a tranquil and natural death. Leave war and strife behind you; dwell in peace; conduct yourselves like men; let there be no quarrelling amongst you, but build up a great people."

It is in the biographical records of noted individuals that we meet with the most pleasing presentations of Maori character and customs. There we find the mask of ferocity and heartless cruelty which the tyranny of custom obliged the Maori to wear in his public intercourse with his fellow-men, laid aside, and the real man, with his human sympathies and feelings, revealed to us. There we find the domestic life of the people stripped of its repulsive features, and presenting a picture which civilized men can look upon with pleasure. One of the most charming specimens of this kind of literature is the story of Hinemoa, the maiden of Rotorua. The story tells how the beautiful maiden, who lived on the shores of Lake Rotorua, and the young chief Tutanekai, who lived on an island in the lake, fell in love with each other; how for a long time each suffered from the secret fear that the other might not share the affection felt. It describes the joy which followed the discovery that it was mutual, and the precautions taken by the young lady's friends to prevent her escape. It tells how the youth nightly serenaded his lady-love from a tower on his island-home, and how the sounds of his flute borne over the water so affected her that she could not endure separation from him; and on a dark night, guided by the sound of her lover's flute, she swam across to Mokoia. At the spot where Hinemoa landed was a hot spring. She got into it to warm herself, for she was trembling all over, partly from the cold after swimming across the lake, and partly from modesty at the thought of meeting Tutanekai. Whilst warming herself a slave came close to her to draw water from the lake. The maiden, who was very frightened, called out in an assumed voice, "For whom is that water?" "Tutanekai," was the reply. This was a good omen for her, and she bethought herself of a device to bring her lover to her side. Calling to the servant, she said, "Give me a drink." When the calabash was handed to her she purposely let it fall on a rock, and broke it. The servant returned for another, but he had no sooner filled it than she again asked for a drink, and when the calabash was handed to her she dropped it on the rock, and broke it. This was repeated several times. The slave thought it best to report the matter to his master, who on hearing what had happened seized a weapon and hurried down to the bath, where he shouted, "Where is that fellow who broke my calabashes?"

The charming simplicity and naturalness with which the conflicting feelings of modesty and love surging in the maiden's bosom are described in this concluding part of the story invest it with singular beauty. There is an entire absence of anything indelicate, or calculated to wound in the slightest degree the susceptibilities of the most sensitive and refined. Hinemoa (says the story) knew the voice; the sound of it was that of the beloved of her heart; and she hid herself under the overhanging rocks of the hot spring. But her hiding was hardly a real hiding, but rather a bashful concealing of herself from Tutanekai. He went feeling about along the banks of the hot spring, searching everywhere, while she coyly hid under the ledges of the rock, peeping out, wondering when she would be found. At last he caught hold of her

hand, and cried out, "Ah! who is this?" And
Hinemoa answered, "It is I, Tutanekai." But
he said, "But who are you? "It is I; it is
Hinemoa." And he said, "Ho! ho! ho! Can
such, in very truth, be the case!" And she
answered, "Yes." And

> She rose up in the water
> As beautiful as the wild white hawk,
> And stepped on the edge of the bath
> As graceful as the shy white crane.

"And he threw his garment over her, and they proceeded to his home, and she became his wife."

*The chief who committed this tradition to writing winds it up with the following words: "Never yet have the lips of the offspring of Hinemoa forgotten to repeat the tale of the great beauty of their renowned ancestress, and her brave deed in swimming over the lake to Mokoia." And, we may add, nor will the race that has succeeded to their inheritance at Rotorua cease to cherish the memory of that romantic story, which will for ever grace the pages of this country's history.

Another charming story is that of Te Ponga's love for Puhihuia:—

The tribes of Waikato were at war with the tribes who occupied the country around Auckland Harbour. Battle after battle was fought without any advantage being secured by either side. Wearied out at last, they mutually agreed to make peace, and one of the fiercest of

---
*See Sir George Grey's letter in the Preface.

the Waikato warriors undertook to arrange the terms. Accompanied by a large force he entered the enemy's fortress, which occupied the summit and slopes of Mount Eden. He was welcomed in the usual manner, and after the complimentary speeches were over a great feast was held. In the evening the residents entertained their visitors by dancing and singing before them. The young daughter of the chief of the town, watching a good opportunity, bounded forward to display her skill in dancing. The strangers were overpowered by her beauty, and Te Ponga, their leader, "felt his heart grow wild with emotion when he saw so much loveliness before him." The visitors, in their turn, gave an exhibition of their skill, on which occasion Te Ponga acquitted himself with such grace as to win Puhihuia's admiration. A passionate attachment sprang up between the two. Te Ponga, unable to sleep for his great love for the maiden, lay tossing all night from side to side, devising scheme after scheme by which he might secure a private interview with the maiden and disclose to her his love. His slave, noticing his restlessness, sought the cause; and, on being told, made the following suggestion: "To-morrow, at nightfall, as you sit in the courtyard of your host, feign to be very thirsty, and call loudly for me to fetch you some water. I will keep well away; and do you continue to shout angrily to me, 'I want water. Fetch me water.' Call so that the father of the young girl may hear, and he will certainly tell her to fetch you some. Then, rise and follow her as if in search of me." Te Ponga carried out his servant's suggestion, which resulted as he had anticipated. Pretending to search for his servant, that he might administer a beating for his prolonged absence, Te Ponga followed Puhihuia. He had no knowledge of the path to the spring; but, directed by the voice of the maiden, who tripped along singing merrily, he reached the fountain just as she was dipping her calabash into it. Hearing footsteps behind her, Puhihuia turned quickly round, and there stood Te Ponga himself. She was too startled and astonished to speak for some moments, and when she recovered herself she asked, "What can have brought you here?" "I came," he said, "for a draught of water." But the girl replied, "Indeed! did I not come here to draw water for you? Why, then, did you not stay at my father's house until I brought the water to you?" Then Te Ponga answered, "O maiden! you—you are the water that I thirst for." This confession led to a mutual exchange of vows. But they felt that, in consequence of late hostilities between their respective tribes, it would be useless to make their intentions publicly known. It was arranged between them that Puhihuia should elope with Te Ponga on his return. To prevent pursuit, Te Ponga ordered his followers to secretly disable all the war-canoes belonging to their hosts by cutting

the lashings of the topsides. On the morning
the visitors took their departure, Puhihuia left
the pa with a number of her female companions,
and wandered along the path the visitors were
returning by; and, as they came up, she began
joking and laughing with them. Her father,
seeing his daughter and her companions going
so far, called out, "Children, come back here."
All but the chief's daughter at once turned
back; but she had only one thought in her
heart — how to escape with her beloved.
Gliding behind some large scoria rocks, which
hid her movements from the fortress, she
redoubled her speed. Te Ponga, seeing her
running in this hurried manner, called aloud to
his men to follow. " Then began a swift flight
indeed—of Te Ponga, and his warriors, and the
young girl. Rapidly they flew, like feathers
drifting before the gale, or as runs the weka
which has broken loose from the fowler's snare.
When the chief of Maungawhau saw that his
daughter would be lost, he called upon his
people to pursue her. There was a wild rushing
to and fro for weapons, which delayed the
pursuers, who reached the beach at Manukau
just as Te Ponga had embarked with the
maiden in his war-canoe. His men dashed
their paddles into the water, and shot away
swift as a dart from a sling;" and, like Lord
Ullin, the father of Puhihuia was left on the
shore lamenting.

Besides these tales of love of which I have
just given specimens, there are many fairy tales,

and tales of magic and sorcery — tales of monsters that dwelt in deep pools, and in caves and forests.

Sir George Grey has preserved two specimens of Maori fairy tales which bear a strong family likeness to similar stories found in Europe and elsewhere. The first tells how the art of netting was discovered by a certain chief, who found the fairies one night drawing their fishing-nets on the coast near the North Cape. He joined them, and, by delaying their departure till dawn, secured their nets, and so learnt the stitch, and taught his descendants. The other story relates how a hunting-party on the Waikato were terrified by fairies, who swarmed all round their camp-fire, climbing over the roots of the trees to peep at Te Kanawa, who, to propitiate their good-will, presented his greenstone and other ornaments. "The fairies, contenting themselves with the shadows of the ornaments, retired before dawn."

The fairies are described as a numerous people, merry, cheerful, and always singing, diminutive in person, with fair hair and skin. Upwards of forty years ago I used to hear the Maoris continually talking about the doings of the fairies, and often met persons who declared they had seen them. One man described how he saw the fairies building a pa on the summit of a hill enveloped in mist. From the way he told his story I felt sure he had actually seen what he was describing, but probably what he took to be fairies were the shadows of men building a pa at some distance, thrown upon the curtain of mist.

Some of the stories of sorcery and magic are very curious. On Banks Peninsula, near Gough's Bay, the trees were thought to be enchanted men, and able at times to move about. Sorcerers were said to have the power of striking people dead by a look, and withering up trees and shrubs. Persons of ignoble birth or unskilled in magic were warned never to look upon any enchanted object for fear of losing their sight or their lives.

The legend of the magical wooden head explains how sorcerers accomplished their ends. The story throws some light upon the ideas prevalent amongst the Maoris regarding the manner in which supernatural aid was to be obtained, to enable men to accomplish what was beyond the ordinary power of mortals. A celebrated sorcerer who lived in ancient times, possessed a magical wooden head which caused the death of all who came within a certain distance of it without the owner's permission. A brave warrior renowned for skill in magic resolved to rid the country of the pest. To gain his object, he enlisted by the agency of powerful charms and incantations the services of thousands of spirits kindly disposed to mankind, to fight the malignant spirits who guarded the head. A battle ensued, the evil spirits were defeated, the fortress was taken, and the cruel sorcerer and owner of the magical head was put to death.

SPECIMENS OF STERN-POSTS.

Maori fables (says Mr. Colenso, in his able paper, Vol. I., Trans. N.Z. Inst.) are very natural and correct, and mostly conversational, between animals or natural objects, such as between the large rock-lizard and the red gurnet, the codfish and the fresh-water eel, the rat and the green paroquet, the sweet potato and the fern-root. Had they more and larger animals they might have had a volume of fables rivalling those of Æsop.

Their legends of ogres and monsters are very like the stories that still linger in European nurseries. They are said to have been the first occupants of this country. They are described as gaints who could stride from mountain-range to mountain-range, swallow rivers, and transform themselves into anything, animate or inanimate, that they chose.

But there is a still more remarkable class of legends, relating to the existence of huge reptiles of the saurian order, which are said to have infested various parts of this country, and to have proved very destructive to the inhabitants. The descriptions given of the appearance of these huge reptiles, and their habits, and the manner in which they were captured, are so minute and exact that it is hard to believe that the accounts relating to them are of such great antiquity as the evidence we possess proves them to be. For it appears that these legends are common to all branches of the Maori race. Judge Fornander, referring to these *taniwha* stories, in the first volume of his interesting work on the Polynesian race, says, "The Hawaiian legends frequently speak of reptiles of extraordinary size, living in caverns, amphibious in their nature, and being the terror of the inhabitants Now, when it is taken into consideration that throughout the Polynesian groups no reptiles are found much larger than the common lizard, it is evident that these tales of monster reptiles must have been an heirloom from the time when the people lived in other habitats, where such large reptiles abounded."

For at least a thousand years these stories have been handed down from generation to generation, and are now told with such minuteness of detail that if we knew nothing about their antiquity we should accept them as descriptions of what happened a comparatively short time ago. The fact of their preservation for so long a period adds greatly to our assurance of the value of such of the Maori traditions as the people themselves assert to be of great antiquity.

The largest collection of Maori poetry is contained in a work, extending over four hundred pages, published in 1853 by Sir George Grey. But this work contains only a portion of the traditional native poetry stored, till Europeans came, in the memories of the people; still, there is quite enough to show how much poetical feeling may coexist with the most revolting usages of a barbarous life. These poems comprise specimens of the various compositions which may be classed under the headings of incantations, visions, and charms; war songs or chants; love songs; canoe songs; historical ballads; dirges, laments; children's songs, lullabies.

Mr. Colenso, remarking upon the poetry of the New Zealander, says, " The people frequently beguiled the monotonous drudgery of some of their heavier work, performed together in company, by songs with suitable choruses. Such songs were sung when dragging or paddling their canoes, or digging in their cultivations. Their war songs and defiances contain horrible curses, and breathe a spirit of ferocity; while their love songs are full of the tenderest feeling, expressed sometimes in the most touching and beautiful language. Their sentimental songs, expressive of abandonment, loneliness, and despair, contain much pathos, and, sung as they always were in a minor key, were often very affecting. The whole of their poetry, though abounding in poetical images, is destitute of rhyme and metre, a deficiency their poets got over by lengthening and shortening vowels and words; proving that the Maoris, like ourselves, conceive of poetry as something far higher than mere versification."

Translators have found great difficulty in getting at the real meaning of many of the compositions, not only owing to the presence in them of obsolete words of great antiquity, but to the extraordinary license allowed to poets in dealing with the words they used. Owing to the peculiar character of the language the omission of a letter might entirely alter the meaning of a word. Take the word "*hanga*," for instance, which means "to make;" omit the "h," and it means "turn," or "facing."

I may be excused for referring here to a note by the Rev. Dr. Maunsell, one of the most learned Maori scholars New Zealand has possessed, on the peculiarities of Maori poetry. Dr. Maunsell says,—

"The construction of Maori poetry was not only abrupt and elliptical to an excess not allowed in English poetry, but it also carries its license so far as to disregard rules of grammar that are strictly observed in prose; alters words so as to make them sound more poetically; deals more arbitrarily with the length of syllables, and sometimes even inverts their order or adds other syllables. It is true that these irregularities help much to invest Maori poetry with that deep shade which none can penetrate without close study of each particular piece; but it must be remembered that by far the largest measure of the difficulty arises from the peculiarly local circumstances, and from the remote and vague allusions so wrought into the piece that even one tribe will often be unable to understand the song of another, especially if it be one of any antiquity.

"To follow the Maori poet through all the wild irregularities of his flight would be far from the intention of these notes. .... They will be found for the most part to consist of omissions of the nominative case, of the objective, often of the verb and verbal particles, omissions of the prepositions, changes of one preposition into another, unusual words introduced, and words sometimes inverted, exceedingly wild and abrupt metaphors, and transitions unexpected and rapid."

After reading Dr. Maunsell's statement it will not surprise any one to find that much of the Maori poetry baffles all attempts made by Europeans to translate it into intelligible language. The poetry of any language suffers by translation, and in no case is this so apparent as with Maori poetry. Its excellence in the original may be gathered from the fact that, poor as our attempts at translation are, they will be found to contain much that is beautiful in sentiment and expression.

The following is a translation of part of an ancient lament by the chief Ika-here-mutu for his children, some of whom died in battle, others of disease. (For original see Sir G. Grey's "Poetry of the New Zealanders," page 9.)

Here I sit, while my throbbing heart
Mourns for my loved children.
Here, like Tane's offspring,
Drooping yonder in the inland forest,
I bend like the fronds of the tree-fern
    Over my lost children.
Where art thou, O my son!
Thou whom thy people were wont to greet

With the welcome cry, "Draw near! Draw near!"
Thou art gone, alas!
Borne by the strong ebbing tide
[That bears all men away].
O my friends! here I sit alone
Upon the plot where my flock gathered—
A slippery plot,* swept so clean
That nothing now remains to greet mine eyes.
I cannot bear to gaze upon the sun
Now shining down on me.
[Its bright light mocks the darkness of my soul.]
I cannot bear to gaze on Taranaki's snowy peak,
Nor to feel the warm inland breeze blow upon my cheek,
For they only serve to wake the memory of my loss.

Trees were called the offspring of Tane, as he was father of all vegetation. The shape and appearance of the tree-fern affords a beautiful and appropriate simile to describe the attitude of the broken-hearted father, with bowed head and extended arms, bending over the remains of his children after Maori custom.

Hinewhe's Lament for her father, Te Rauparaha, when carried off by a Man-of-war Crew.†

[Te Rauparaha, the celebrated northern chief, who was residing with his family on the shores Porirua Harbour, was unexpectedly seized and carried off one night by a man-of-war crew, as he was suspected of treacherous intentions towards the settlers at Wellington. His daughter is very satirical in her allusions to those who preached peace and practised treachery.]

Love no longer burns within the breasts
[Of your once-famed warrior tribe].

---
*The slippery plot, literally—the sea swept rocks where the sea-birds flock together.
†See Sir G. Grey's "Poetry of the New Zealanders" page 12.

Kapti's summit stands alone,
For thou, the famous of the land,
   Art snatched away.
Sleep, warrior, sleep on shipboard,
And then you may be bound, spirit of the deep.
   *   *   *   *   *   *
The rata-tree that grew beside me,
That sheltered me with its spreading boughs,
Is gone—torn from the midst of Toa's sons—
   Of Toa the brave.
Why were you not snatched away
When the eyes were bloodshot in battle?
From the mouth of the loaded gun
You might then have cried,
   "Comrades, farewell,
   Night's shadows close around."
But who can turn life's stream,
Or fetch its waters back!
   'Tis past, 'tis past.
Revenge alone remains.
Your grandsons, they shall seek it;
For your own sons and followers lie
Like lazy kokopu in darkling pools asleep.
Farewell, my father,
Offering made by Tamihana and Matene to the god of peace.
Alas! from realms below was brought this treacherous law.
The law they promised us was one of peace.
My faults alone have ruined you.

Kapiti was Te Rauparaha's stronghold. His son Tamihana and his nephew Matene introduced Christianity to the tribe called Toa, or the "brave." Trusting to the peaceful professions of the English, Te Rauparaha took no precautions to protect himself, and was easily taken prisoner. The news of his capture roused the indignation of his daughter, who is unsparing in her ridicule of the cowardice of Toa's sons, and the treachery of the English under the guise of peace.

An Exile's Lament for his Native Land.

Afar the tide of Kawhia laps the shore.
Alas! we are parted now.
Over the well-known hills
The clouds are creeping slowly up to me,
To pass over me, and join me to thee.
    Land of my childhood,
    Here, from afar, I greet thee.

The Lament of One forsaken in her Old Age by her Husband.

Sink, O sun! Descend to thy cave,
And carry tidings there.
    Alas! Alas!
Like the flood-tide returning ever,
The tears rise in my eyelids,
But thou repliest not.
    Alas! Alas!
The smoke is just now rising from the south.
'Tis there Ngawhare dwells, the man I love.
Why didst thou lead me thus far,
To fling me, like rejected food, aside?
'Twas thou, with smooth, deceitful words,
Didst lure me from my home.
With lightsome step I followed thee.
   *   *   *   *
Oh! why did I scorn Te Wheoro,
Betrothed in infancy to me?
   *   *   *   *
'Tis now the seventh moon,
The time when
The white flowers of the "toe" bloom [on me]:
The eighth month comes, and they are blown away.
    Alas! Alas!
The rainbow stands above, the lightnings flash,
And I depart.
    Alas! Alas!

A Lover's Lament.

The mists still hang on Pukehina.
Along its slopes my lover wends his way.
Turn, love, once more,
That I may pour forth my tears to thee.
I was not the first to speak of love.
You deceived me, your inferior;
And now my foolish heart
Is beside itself
When my eyes rest, love, on thee.

The following translation is taken from Mr. Colenso's paper in Vol. XIII., Trans. N.Z. Inst., p. 75 :—

A Love Chant.

Rain on, O thou rain! Continue to rain down without there. Here am I within the hut deploring my distress, and comparing [this with that]; for my eyes are as if supplied with water from a flowing spring. It is the great love I bear to the fond one of my affection that causes these fiery, convulsive pains—the dear one, who is so greatly desired and longed-for. Now, alas! thou art separated far off to a distance, who will return thee hither to me? . . . . I will go forth to look at the fleecy clouds sailing hither, coming this way over the mountain. Alas! the boundary that parts us, dear young lady, is as a great ocean-depth to thee. Notwithstanding in that one direction — towards thee—my eyes are dim with steady gazing; for thou alone art the only one of my deepest affection. . . . .

A Love Song by a Widow for her Deceased Husband.

After the evening hours
I recline upon my bed.
Thy own spirit-like form
Comes towards me,
Creeping stealthily along.

Alas! I mistake,
Thinking thou art here with me,
Enjoying the light of day.
Then, the affectionate remembrances
Of the many days of old
Keep on rising within my heart.
This, however, loved one—
This thou must do:
Recite the potent call to Rakahua,
And the strong cry to Rikiriki,
That thou mayest return.
For thou wast ever more than a common husband—
Thou wast my best-beloved, my chosen,
My treasured possession. Alas!

A Love Song.

Rise up quickly, O thou moon!
Make haste to get above me,
That I may give vent to my sighing
And utter my laments.
Now, indeed, for the first time
I feel the pangs of love.
It is as if a demon or a lizard
Were within me gnawing.

* * * *

O ye light, fleecy clouds flitting above!
Fly on, fly away, and carry tidings,
That my beloved one may hear of me in her anxiety.

* * * *

Alas! alas! my very eyesight
Is fast failing me:
When I look at the distant headlands
They quiver, and are dim.

The PROVERBS were very numerous, and afford abundant evidence of the wit and shrewdness of the people. Nothing pleased a Maori audience better than to hear them aptly quoted.

Unfortunately, some of the best would be almost unintelligible to English people; but the following specimens will be understood and appreciated :—

How often does the weka escape the snare! (Equivalent to our proverb, " A burnt child dreads the fire ")

The white crane, whose flight is seen but once. (Equivalent to " Angels' visits, few and far between.")

The road to Hawaiki is cut off. The tide fills the Cave of Death of the Hundred Seamonsters. (Equivalent to " The Rubicon is passed.")

Black and red united can do it. (The red-ochred chief and charcoal-smeared slave united can do anything.)

Food given by another person is only a throat-tickler; but food gained by the labour of one's own hand is the food which satisfies.

A man fond of sleep and a man fond of idleness will never obtain wealth.

The passing clouds can be seen; but passing thoughts cannot be seen.

Great is your going forth (to war); small your return. (Equivalent to Ahab saying to Benhadad—1 Kings, xx., 2- " Let not him that girdeth on his armour boast.")

Deep throat: shallow muscle. (An idle glutton.)

He who goes before gathers treasures; he who lags behind looks for them in vain.

Sir, bale the water out of your mouth.
(Equivalent to vulgar colonialism, " Dry up.")

Dropping water wears away the soil; so frequent slander a good name.

Perhaps thou camest hither from the village of Mr. Falseways. Perhaps thou and Take-up-talk travelled hither together.

One day's beauty, a short-lived pleasure. (Sometimes used of a girl's countenance.)

Show yourself a true man, never be disobedient.

Food underdone is your own; fully cooked goes to others. (A warning to dawdlers.)

Totara forehead. (Equivalent to "Brazen-face.")

The following specimen of epistolary composition, which came accidentally into my possession, shows how naturally Maoris express their thoughts in poetical language. The writer is a very commonplace-looking old man, who came from the North Island to reside at Kaiapoi some years ago. He is the last person any European would imagine capable of expressing himself in the way he does here :—" Nau mai haere atu ra e taku karere aroha i runga i nga huamo nunui o nga ngaru nunui o te moana tutuki atu ki nga Roma kino o Raukawa. Ma ' Te Anau ' koe e mau atu ki Kihipone. Ma te mera koe e hari atu ki te poutapeta i Tokomaru. Ma tetahi tangata koe e mau atu kia Tamara raua ko Heni, me nga tamariki hoki. E hika ma, tena koutou." [Come hither, and go, my messenger of love, on the great rearing crests of the mighty heaving billows of the ocean, that meet the angry waves of the stormy Straits of Raukawa (Cook Strait). The "Te Anau" will convey you to Gisborne. The mail will carry you to the post-office at Tokomaru, and some person will carry you to Damaris and Jane, and to their children. Ladies, I salute you and your children!]

Even this brief and superficial survey of Maori traditions furnishes sufficient evidence to prove that they are something more than mere literary curiosities, and that in proportion as they become better known to ethnologists their value will be more fully realised and understood.

The fact that they contain myths relating to the origin of all things corresponding in details and in chronological order with those of the Homeric age, must tend to remove doubts as to the possibility of knowledge being transmitted for ages by oral tradition; for in no other way have the Maoris preserved those myths which they possess in common with races from whom they have been separated for probably not less than two thousand years, and which were evidently derived from a common source.

In the poetry and proverbs of this long-isolated people we find the same ideas and the same similies employed that the poets and sages of the Old World used to describe human passions and emotions, and to sum up the thoughts of the wise; and we find their orators giving utterance in their public speeches to lofty ideas, in strange contrast with their sordid surroundings. But, as beseems an antipodean literature, some of the ideas are found to be topsy-turvy. In place of Aphrodite, it is the hero Maui who rises from the foam of the sea ; it is Hinemoa who swims the strait, and not Leander ; and, instead of the angels falling in love with female beauty, it is the manly beauty of Tawhaki that attracts the celestial fair one from her heavenly home.

So far from being ignorant savages, we find that a large proportion of the people possessed cultivated minds, and were well-instructed in subjects which only highly-educated Europeans think of acquiring any exact knowledge about. They were familiar with the flora and fauna of their country, to every object of which they gave distinctive names,* precise enough to prove that they were keen and intelligent observers of all natural objects. They scanned the stars and named the various constellations, and took such note of their movements as to mark the seasons by them. Their sense of beauty was so correct that, simple as their clothing, and utensils, and weapons were, they designed the forms of them in such a way as to render them objects of beauty. With such inferior tools as sharp fragments of stone and shells, their artists executed with

---

*See " Forest Flora," by Kirk ; and Buller's " Birds ; " and Colenso's papers in Trans. N.Z. Inst.

finished workmanship carvings of complicated pattern and beautiful design. Possessing that subtle faculty which enables people to discern at once the fitness of things, the Maoris preserved in the formal intercourse with each other the utmost propriety of conduct, and always behaved with dignified self-possession in the presence of civilised men, however exalted in station.

Those who only fix their eyes upon the defective side of the Maori's character and acquirements; who think only of his cruel behaviour towards his foes and inferiors, and forget his courtesy and generosity to his friends and equals; who think only of the things in which he comes behind the ordinary civilised man, instead of the things in which he excelled him, will find in these traditions a rebuke administered to that spirit of race-pride which leads the European to look with feelings akin to contempt on all coloured men, as if they were all alike infinitely beneath him; and they will also learn how it is that most of those Europeans who have taken pains to acquire accurate knowledge of the first inhabitants of this country have formed such a high opinion of the Maori race.

SITUATION OF PLACES MENTIONED.

Ao-tea-roa	North Island.
Apa'rima	Name of Jacobs river.
Ara'hura	A river on the West Coast.
Ha'tai'tai	Pa near entrance Wellington Harbour.
Kani'ere	Mountain near source of Waimakariri.
Kapuka'riki	Cust.
Kapara'te'hau	Near Cape Campbell.
Kai'hinu	Mountain on shores of Tory Channel.
Kura'te'au	Tory Channel.
Kai'apoh'ia	
Kura-tawhiti	Part of Mt. Torlesse Range.
Kou'kou'rarata	Port Levy.
Maunga'tere	Mt. Grey.
Moi'oio	Island in Tory Channel.
Mai'rangi	Cust Downs.
Mata'ki'kai'poika	Pa on S. East Coast North Island.
Ma'tau	Molyneux.
Nga'toko'ono	Pa between Gough's and Long Bay, Banks Peninsula.
O'te'kaue	Pa at mouth of Wairua.
O'mihi	Pa near Hau muri Bluff.
Ohou	Near Opihi.
Okohana	Church bush, Kaiapoi.
Ote'poti	Port Chalmers.
Para'kakariki	Pa near Long Bay, Banks Peninsula.
Pa'kihi	Pa South of Hau muri.
Peke'ta	Pa South of Hau muri.
Puke'kura	Taiaroa Head, Otago.
Pio'pio'tahi	Milford Sound.
Raki'ura	Stewarts Island.
Rau'kawa	Cook's Strait.
Tumuki	South Island, afterwards Waipounamu.
Ta'wera	Mt. Torlesse.
Tete'whai	Battle ground near Waipapa.
Tutae'puta'puta	River South of Hau muri.
Tara'hau'kapiti	Mountain near Jacobs river.

Tau'mutu	Mouth of Lake Ellesmere.
Tu'hua	Mayor Island.
Taiari	River in Otago.
Upoko'pipi	Pa near Arowhenua.
Whanga'nui'a'tara	Wellington Harbour.
Wai'para	River in North Canterbury.
Wai'mea	River near Nelson.
Wai'hopai	New River, Southland.
Wai'hora	Lake Ellesmere, Canterbury, and Waihola in Otago.
Wai'kou'aiti	River in Otago.
Whata'a'rama	Part of Mt. Torlesse Range.
Wai'kakahi	Wascoes, Banks Peninsula.
Wai'tangi	River in Canterbury.
Wai'tara'mea	Stream in Southland.

www.ingramcontent.com/pod-product-compliance
Lightning Source LLC
Chambersburg PA
CBHW020101170426
43199CB00009B/363